Murder on the Llano Estacado

by Marlowe J. Churchill

DORRANCE
PUBLISHING CO
EST. 1920
PITTSBURGH, PENNSYLVANIA 15238

Dorrance Publishing Co
585 Alpha Drive
Pittsburgh, PA 15238
Visit our website at *www.dorrancebookstore.com*

ISBN: 979-8-88812-239-6
eISBN: 979-8-88812-739-1

"[West Texas] is a paradise for men and dogs, and a hell for women and horses."
—*New York Evangelist*, 5 June 1884, p. 2

Prairie madness or **prairie fever** was an affliction that affected settlers in the Great Plains during the migration to, and settlement of, the Canadian Prairies and the Western United States in the nineteenth century. Settlers moving from urbanized or relatively settled areas in the east faced the risk of mental breakdown caused by the harsh living conditions and the extreme levels of isolation on the prairie. Symptoms of prairie madness included depression, withdrawal, changes in character and habit, and violence. Prairie madness sometimes resulted in the afflicted person moving back east, or in extreme cases, suicide.

Prairie madness is not a clinical condition, rather it is a pervasive subject in writings of fiction and non-fiction from the period to describe a fairly common phenomenon. It was described by Eugene Virgil Smalley in 1893: "an alarming amount of insanity occurs in the new Prairie States among farmers and their wives."[1][2]

To my mother, Bonnie Belle Churchill, whose memories of this family tragedy prompted my writing this narrative.

Table of Contents

PROLOGUE

Traffic was backed up at the railroad crossing that connects Farwell, Texas, and Texico, New Mexico, two tiny towns that, more than a hundred years ago, competed fiercely for the wages of cowboys anxious to take a load off after weeks in the saddle. Waiting for the freight train pulling more than 100 graffiti-stained boxcars to clear the crossing, I was eager to finally visit the place I had imagined for years, the place where my great aunt Susan Ferguson Hassell and eight of her children were murdered one by one just before Christmas 1926 as they slept. It was a grisly crime that would shock the nation. But there would be many more grisly murders to shock Americans in the years following, and my family's tragedy would be forgotten for the most part, except for a few in my family who sought details about what had become a family secret. As my elders passed away, I found myself asking questions that nobody in my family knew much about, and there were few documents available to plumb for information. I was on a mission to find out what had happened in Farwell that so bedeviled my mother to the day she died and now was consuming me. I had always doubted my mom's curious story about my great aunt.

Mom and I had a stressful relationship after I started school, probably because she was a hovering mother who worried about me getting dirty playing in the yard and preferred me playing the piano over my preference of football and baseball.

Due to the tension between us, youthful arrogance, and inconsistencies in some of her tales, I began doubting her stories of being able to ride a horse like a jockey and all her fanciful references to ranching and the Old West of cowboys and Indians. Once I saw my mom in her prim dress climb onto a picnic table to escape a curious horse that had interrupted our picnic lunch by nudging her for a treat. My father came to her rescue and shooed the animal away, reprimanding me for laughing instead of helping her. I remember thinking, why would a person raised on a ranch be afraid of animals? And a person who had the skills of a jockey would not need rescuing from a horse.

Her vague tale of a homicide in the family seemed to me to be utterly fanciful, or perhaps a gross exaggeration. I admit that again, due to my stubbornness and our tenuous relationship, I decided it was another of my mother's tall tales. I never really asked her any questions about it.

She continued to lose credibility with me as I grew older and continued to doubt her tales, and I pulled away from her as she began to hover over my little sister instead. There's a saying I heard from Pulitzer-Prize-winning investigative journalist Bob Greene of Long Island, New York's, *Newsday,* that described how journalists think: "If your mother says she loves you, check it out." And so after I retired, I did. When Mom died, I decided a good project would be digging for the real story about the supposed homicide. I knew only the barest of details. I knew the first name of a victim, whom my mother knew as "Aunt Susie."

Just as the westbound train cleared the tracks, it revealed the caboose of a passing eastbound train. Both trains left the crossing at the same time in opposite directions, and there, from the windshield of my rented Wrangler, was my first glimpse of the town of Farwell, Texas. I felt great excitement, like the curtains were parting just before the movie would begin. A tall grain silo dominated the town. I couldn't wait to see more.

Entrance to Farwell, Texas

Here was a place that had lured Aunt Susie, her children, and her new husband to relocate from Oklahoma and begin a new life on the Llano Estacado—country flatter than flat, so empty, beautiful in a subdued, desolate fashion. The Spanish name for the region roughly translates as "Staked Plains," and folklore tells of early Mexican and Spanish explorers who poked stakes into the flat ground to mark their way into the unknown, so they could safely return.

I knew that the murder site was a mile east of town. I could not wait for directions. After an unsuccessful attempt to find the house on my own, I reluctantly drove back into town. The courthouse and jail were my next immediate objective, and I was astounded to see the historic brick courthouse—the very courthouse I would soon discover was the scene of the most famous murder trial West Texas had ever witnessed. Standing near the courthouse was a two-story abandoned building: it was the jail I had been told had confined the killer.

Farwell was waiting for me.

Historic Parmer County Courthouse where Hassell trial convened

Farwell's old jail where Hassell was confined

Christmas Eve, 1926

Early Christmas Eve morning, just past four o'clock, Lindop (first name unknown) heard something in another part of the small farmhouse. To him it was still an unfamiliar home with unfamiliar noises, and there was a guest sleeping in another room—a guest who had been acting rather odd in the past few days. He had been withdrawn and sullen when eating dinner with Lindop and his family.

A faint noise, perhaps the rustling of his restless guest unable to sleep, came from the guest's room. Lindop and his family were still recovering from the big move out of their previously rented farmhouse a mile away to this rental house. His family was taking over the rental from a fellow farmer, the man in the guest room, who was pulling up stakes and moving on from Farwell.

Although the lease was now theirs, Lindop and his wife had agreed to let their guest remain in the bedroom for a few more days, so he could finish cleaning it and packing his last belongings while wrapping up his local business and before rejoining his family, whom folks heard had moved back to Oklahoma. It was an awkward time, with him broodingly sharing dinner with the Lindops and their boys and the baby, then retiring to his room about nine o'clock every night.

The house was cold when Lindop first heard the noise, and his wife figured Hassell might be trying to start a fire. She told her husband to go get the fire going, knowing Hassell would not be able to figure out how to operate their stove, which they had brought with them in the move. So Lindop got out of bed and got a good fire roaring to heat the house before hearing their guest summon him for help.

Hassell had sold everything he owned at an auction that had brought lots of people into the Lindops' new home and backyard in the days before Christmas. There was something about him that made Lindop uneasy. When the Lindops had toured the house before deciding to rent it, Hassell had stood in the guest room doorway and adamantly refused to let Lindop and his wife check out the room. Lindop would later testify to this in court. Hassell had made an excuse that he was still cleaning the room and it still housed some of his belongings. In hindsight Lindop would remember that moment and wonder.

Lindop tapped on the guest room door, which quickly opened. Hassell asked Lindop to get a doctor, so with no inquiry into the problem, Lindop awakened one of his sons and dispatched him to bring the doctor. With no idea what was going on, Lindop checked on Hassell again; Hassell remained quiet. Lindop never described what he saw inside the room nor the appearance of the man seeking his help; in short order, his wounds would be discovered. The third time Lindop ventured into the room, Hassell asked quietly if the doctor had been summoned.

Told the doctor was being called, Hassell then said, "Bring Jim Martin."

"Who is Jim Martin?" Lindop asked.

"The sheriff," Hassell replied.

Lindop later said he was so concerned at that point that he got his wife and family into their Ford at about 4:30 in the morning and drove the short distance to Judge James Hamlin's home. Hamlin owned the home Lindop was now renting and owned a good portion of the rest of Farwell, too. His wife, Kate, oversaw the business of their rental properties. Hamlin called Sheriff Martin at Lindop's request.

When Lindop returned to the farmhouse later that morning, the backyard was crowded with people digging in and standing around a big pit. It was a crime scene, but in 1926, there was no plastic yellow police tape to protect what police were beginning to uncover and no understanding of securing the site. People were trampling all over it.

And that's when everything changed in Farwell, Texas. In 1926 the joy of Christmas was overshadowed by an unspeakable horror.

George Hassell, executed in 1928 for murdering two families. Photo provided by Lana Payne Barnett.

Sheriff Martin and the county attorney were already familiar with the wounded man, George Hassell, and his family. Some of his neighbors had recently reported suspicions regarding the whereabouts of Hassell's family. In fact the sheriff and county attorney had interviewed Hassell and had been waiting on confirmation that Susie Hassell and her eight children were where the man had said they had gone. During that interview, Hassell reacted to the questions about his family as if it were nobody's business but his.

The Lindop home was abuzz with activity. The noise of shovels chopping into the cold ground, the crowd's anticipation of what might be unearthed. The biting cold made the work and wait all that much harder. Men would later testify about the freezing sleet they experienced as they toiled in the early-morning darkness. Mini clouds formed with each breath they exhaled.

The moment the men with shovels found the first sign of Hassell's missing family was shocking for these farm folk, who to that point had led quiet lives raising livestock and crops, tending to their families, and looking forward to a new year that might bring a bit more prosperity.

Word quickly spread about the horrible scene behind the Lindops' new home. The local historical society later commissioned a history of Farwell. That Christmas was remembered with this entry:

> "As the year 1926 drew to a close, the inhabitants of Farwell were getting ready for a big Christmas. Crops had been good, cattle prices were high, and the farmers and

ranchers were in a holiday mood. They were unaware that tragedy had struck their community once again."

(The previous tragedy was a huge arson fire that had devastated the downtown.)

I don't remember when I first heard about my Great Aunt Susie. Certainly it was not from my grandmother, Susie's youngest sister. Grandmother was a quiet, stern woman who was always very busy cooking and caring for my family on our biannual visits to her home in Colorado. My grandfather had Parkinson's disease, and I couldn't understand the words he mumbled from his bed, where he spent most of his last days. I treasured a photograph of him as a teenaged rancher courting my grandmother, driving a matched pair of white horses pulling a shiny black carriage.

Author's mother, and granddaughter Tiffany Anne

My mother, born Bonnie Bell Beagle to Ethel and Forrest Beagle in Perryton, Texas in 1916, did a lot of talking when I was growing up. She was a great conversationalist and storyteller, who regaled my little sister and me with stories of being a child of the Western frontier, the same frontier of Zane Grey novels. She was Grandmother's sole daughter in a family of five rugged and tall sons who all fought in World War II and Korea. Grandmother doted on her, teaching her the things wives needed to know in those days.

Once, while walking home from school, Mom and a younger brother were kidnapped near their Colorado ranch by a man desperate to ransom them. Miraculously he released them unharmed hours later. Her kidnapping became a story we heard frequently. Although as I grew older, I tended to listen to Mom's many stories with skepticism, I do believe this kidnapping actually occurred. My grandparents were well-off, and a botched kidnapping for ransom was more than conceivable to me.

Mom was sent off to college in California for an education while her brothers were either high school drop-outs or lucky to graduate before enlisting in the military. They later raised families on the wages of blue-collar work. In her early twenties, Mom became a school teacher in a tiny, rural school house west of Montrose and near Grand Junction, Colorado. She would leave her teaching career when Dad returned from fighting in World War II to raise her two kids.

Her grade-school students, the kidnapping incident, her Shetland pony, and the Native Americans who visited their ranch and camped beside the creek when she was young were the stories repeated time and again as the four of us traveled from one military base to another during my dad's Air Force service. I wanted to listen to the radio, but Mom insisted on silence, so she could reminisce uninterrupted.

Once as we passed through her birthplace—I must have been seven or eight—her memories prompted the first narrative about Aunt Susie. For the first time, I heard the word *murder* when she spoke of my aunt. I listened intently to her words of her aunt being murdered, but she never added that others were also killed or where and when this all occurred. It was as if she were recounting events the way the ten-year-old she had been would have.

From then on, this story would be repeated whenever Mom heard mention of either Texas or some other gruesome crime. I do not recall any other details that Mom shared about the murder, and I just wonder whether I was tired of hearing the story and skeptical and tuned out other details. My sister believes our grandparents shielded Mom from many details when she became obsessed with the murders and possibly slipped into depression and forbade Mom from bringing up the story again. There never seemed to be a complete story that made any sense to me, and maybe in retrospect, Mom simply did not know much more than she shared with us. When her mind darkened with dementia, a story of her grandfather being advised by a lynch mob to tip his hat if he wanted the mob to lynch the killer became her mantra as I sat with her at a nursing home and watched her wither away. Just before her death in 2012, I asked her where this murder occurred and the name of the killer. By then it was too late for her to help me understand.

My cousin Sharon Edgar remembers hearing of Aunt Susie's murder from her father (Mom's eldest brother) but never in any detail. Sharon, the eldest of us eighteen cousins, heard her grandparents, her uncles, and perhaps my mom sitting around a dinner table during a family reunion in Montrose, Colorado, where my grandparents then resided, as they discussed the murder, but she does not remember details. Her sister, Sue, told her that their father discussed the murder with her and her two other sisters after Sharon left home, went to college, and married—never in any detail about what happened but as a worried father understandably concerned about their boyfriends, and later, their spouses.

It was as if my mom's family vowed to keep the details of the tragedy a secret from my generation.

Guilt over my youthful skepticism and stubbornness preventing me from ever drawing out the full story from my mother dogged me for months after her death, and I vowed to uncover the full story. As a newspaperman, I knew how to dig for details. But I also understood that finding documents from nearly 100 years ago would be a challenge.

What was Aunt Susie's last name? Where did this murder occur? And when?

First, I dug up some family history that I thought might include Aunt Susie. Eventually my sister found a genealogy of Mom's family that had been commissioned in the 1960s. One entry revealed the marriage of Susan Ferguson to Thomas Hassell (and nothing else about Thomas) and the names of their nine children. It also included a note about the murder in December 1926, of Susan and eight of her children at the hands of

George Hassell. The date and location of the deaths of my great aunt and her children also were noted. George was not just a murderer, he was a family annihilator.

Upon learning of this horror, I figured George Hassell must have been arrested and his crimes documented in news accounts back in the 1920s. There must have been a trial. But an initial computer search of mass murderers never produced Hassell's name. A letter to Farwell police requesting information resulted in the devastating reply that all records of that era had been lost long ago.

A break came when Texas Tech University's library replied to my request for any documentation of the Christmas 1926, murders with a two-page printout of the Parmer County Historical Society's account of the event, along with several news clippings about the crime.

Life in 1926

What was 1926 like?

It's hard to visualize a time when homes did not include a bathroom or refrigerator. When horses were more reliable transportation than cars. When the nearest telephone might be at a neighbor's home, several miles away.

During the Christmas season of 1926, nobody was expecting a Great Depression in just a few years. Imagine Farwell, Texas in 1926, in those days leading up to Christmas.

Downtown Farwell was the hub for hundreds of folks residing around the area. Most farmers raised livestock they could butcher for food and had cows to provide them with milk. What farmers couldn't grow, raise, or preserve, they could find in the downtown market. Average prices in 1926 included a one-pound tub of butter for forty-nine cents, a pound of sliced ham for forty cents, and pound of coffee for forty-nine cents. A person could order almost anything from the Sears catalog, and I remember my grandmother recalling that the catalog doubled as toilet paper in her home. People stored some perishables outside in dug-outs or earthen cellars.

Cars were becoming more affordable. A Dodge touring car was a bargain at $795. Roads were improving. In November highway officials had assigned a future nearby road the designation U.S. Route 66.

The United States, population 117 million, had observed its 150th birthday on the Fourth of July. Golfer Bobby Jones was the Tiger Woods of the day. The St. Louis Cardinals had whipped the New York Yankees, ending theWorld Series with a tag on second base when Babe Ruth tried to steal. Workers saw a five-day, forty-hour work week, instituted by the Ford Motor Company, on May 1st.

Escape artist Harry Houdini had died. Gangster Al Capone and his gang were at war in Chicago. Actress Greta Garbo was a hit in her movie *Torrent*. Emperor Hirohito was crowned in Japan. Despite the passage of the Nineteenth Amendment allowing women to vote in 1920, they were certainly not being considered for jury duty in any murder trial in 1926.

Another Horror Revealed

Sheriff James Martin's murder suspect George Hassell had attempted suicide—no doubt interrupting Martin's Christmas plans—and was recovering in his jail cell from one serious puncture wound to his stomach and less serious cuts to his wrist (these were self-inflicted early in the morning of December 24th, although Hassell's initial story was that Lindop had attacked him). To the surprise of Martin and his deputies, the suspect was now willing to talk. In addition to granting them a recorded confession to the recent murders, Hassell began talking about a *second* family he had murdered in California years earlier. As you might imagine, I was shocked and horrified, yet deeply intrigued. Hassell was a serial killer?

Just as folks across the nation were looking at maps to identify the location of Farwell, Texas, then came word of murders in another small, obscure town: Whittier in Southern California. The two towns could not be more starkly different. One was once a cowboy town on the dusty Caprock of West Texas, the other was a suburb of Los Angeles with palm-tree-lined streets, almost in the shadow of the Hollywood sign.

When it was that Hassell actually told jailers about the California murders is unclear. The lawmen were suspicious enough about the latest admission of this talkative killer, who thought he could to be friends with everybody, that they contacted the

California city's authorities. Hassell, according to testimony from lawmen, loved to talk, eat, reminisce about his past, and boast of his adventures. He seemed to have nary a care in the world for a man facing capital murder charges and basked in his new-found celebrity.

Telegraph was a quick and common form of communication in 1926. As newspapers all over the nation were carrying stories about this man in Texas who killed his family, the *Whittier News*, always an aggressive small-town newspaper, carried an Associated Press dispatch that mentioned that the prisoner had bragged about killing another wife and children in Whittier, California.

A dispatch from Texas arrived at the Whittier police station soon after Hassell's arrest that said Hassell was boasting of a "perfect crime" he had committed at 236 South Whittier Avenue, in what would nowadays be called Uptown Whittier. The Whittier police were initially stumped by this report of a local family's murder. And privately they were likely humiliated to discover that they had known nothing about a murder within their city limits. They could not find any reference to a George Hassell living in Whittier, and they had no record of any missing woman and her three children, according to news stories in the *Whittier News*. Hassell soon provided them with a map showing the house where he had lived in Whittier.

The first of four stories in the *Whittier News* stated that Hassell had been using the alias of G. G. Baker while residing in Whittier. This same story says authorities were digging at the given address but were still unable to locate anything. The Farwell police next sent a diagram, drawn by Hassell, of a cellar he said he dug beneath the house, where he boasted the bodies were buried five feet below the surface.

Meanwhile one Mrs. George Hoffman of Pittsburgh contacted Whittier's constable in response to the nationwide news accounts about Hassell, a name from her past that she had thought she would never hear again. She told police she had previously sent an inquiry to Whittier authorities in 1917 about her sister, whom she identified as Mrs. J. D. Hassell. She said she had last heard from her sister ten years earlier, when she received a photograph of her and her three children mailed to her by none other than George Hassell. She said her sister was formerly known as Marie Vogel and she believed the children were adopted.

The photograph and letter from Hassell served the intended purpose, it seems, to mollify Mrs. Hoffman and gave Hassell plenty of time to distance himself from the scene of that first crime.

Constable R. B. Way of Whittier was suddenly embroiled in an uncomfortable situation caused by front-page stories, calling into question his abilities. To make matters worse, Mrs. S. C. Shanker, who once lived next door to the Hassells, was quoted in the newspaper saying she and other neighbors had called the police department about a bad odor coming from the house after the Hassells had moved out.

The police came out to investigate, but apparently nothing was done about it, Shanker said.

A now-very-defensive Constable Way confirmed that he had investigated and could find nothing. I can only speculate that

Way was becoming more and more sensitive about his actions on Whittier Avenue as he was hounded by news reporters.

A day after police started digging beneath the house, according to Hassell's diagram, they found the skeletal remains of four people. The woman was identified as Marie Vogel, and her children were identified as George, eight-years-old, an unidentified two-year-old girl, and an unidentified infant. The two younger children had to be autopsied without names.

Constable Way, now under even more pressure, this time from the Los Angeles County Sheriff's Office for his botched earlier investigation, became more defensive and aggressive. He told the newspaper that he had found utility records for the home showing that Hassell was using an alias and that he rented the Whittier house from March 26th, 1917 until August 30th, 1917.

The utility records indicated that the Standard Oil Company employed a man identified as G. G. Baker.

Neighbors who remembered the Baker family recalled that the man now identified as Hassell had said he was moving to San Francisco, but they also thought he had returned to Whittier in 1920. There seems to be no record available to verify that he did in fact return.

What brought Hassell to Southern California and particularly the small town of Whittier?

A possible answer is that Hassell came there to work in the oil fields, something with which he seems to have had experience with in Texas and Oklahoma. California was booming with oil production dating back the 1880s. But why did Hassell use an alias? Was he trying to avoid World War I as a deserter?

Although Hassell had told the utility company he worked for Standard Oil, he could have lied and held any number of jobs as a laborer. But he also could have been on crews boring dry wells all over the region in search of oil. Oil would be discovered near Whittier but long after Hassell had reportedly left town.

It is hard to fathom why Hassell and Marie Vogel chose Whittier to rent a home. Neighbors told authorities they got the impression they were husband and wife and that the three children were their own. It's likely they would have been considered outsiders. And there is nothing to indicate George Hassell was a particularly religious person at that time in a very conservative town.

Whittier was a small city with deep Quaker roots in 1917. Today the city is a sprawling urban area of less than 100,000 people that is coursed by major boulevards and freeways connecting it to other Los Angeles suburbs and the Pacific Ocean to the west.

George Hassell lived among extremely patriotic and conservative people in Whittier as Europe was falling into the chaos of World War I. Southern California men were enlisting to fight in World War I. Quaker men, who opposed all wars, would be excused on religious grounds, and perhaps George felt more secure among Quakers than living in other areas where people might wonder why he wasn't in uniform.

Living as G. G. Baker, Hassell could evade any draft notice. He does not even show up in any U.S. Census. George Hassell was invisible, and he probably preferred keeping that low profile. For a man using an alias, Whittier was the perfect place for him to disappear.

George Hassell remained in Whittier for a spell after burying the bodies of his family. He would later admit to having an affair with a former neighbor and possibly even marrying her.

A Whittier city librarian helped me locate the correct site where Marie Vogel and her children were murdered. I was hoping to find a small bungalow as I drove slowly down Whittier Avenue, checking addresses on the street curbing and the front doors of homes. I knew it was an extremely long shot to find the place. The street numbers had been re-organized over the years, so the exact address Hassell gave to police did not match the numbers I found on the street.

In the end, I was disappointed to find the small house had been demolished years ago and replaced with a modern apartment house. The tree-lined street has plenty of other homes that appear to have been built in the early 1920s or before. The neighborhood is well kept, with bicycles and tricycles parked outside homes with neatly trimmed lawns. I knew it was an extremely long shot to find the original house, but it was fascinating to speculate about finding the real house and knocking on the front door, waiting for the owner or renter to answer. I was prepared to ask if they knew a man had killed a woman and three children in that home in 1917 and buried them in the cellar.

Eventually George left Whittier.

Not much is known about George between the time he resided in Whittier and his appearance on the doorstep of his sister-in-law. Hassell could have used many aliases as he evaded authorities and traveled the country doing odd jobs. The FBI responded to my Freedom of Information Request to search its files and replied that they could find no reports about Hassell gleaned from other police agencies or any subsequent reports of unidentified serial killers or family annihilators. George Hassell may have been an uneducated con man, but he was smart enough to cover his tracks.

Sole Survivor

While the tragedy in Farwell and Whittier dominated the newspapers, little was reported about the lone survivor of the second massacre. Nora, the eldest of the Hassell children, survived the bloodbath because she did not live at the farmhouse. Nora was my mother's older cousin, and according to Mother, Hassell had either telegraphed or called her where she lived in California, requesting that she come immediately to Farwell, declaring that her mother was ill. Nora reportedly was suspicious of the summons but did make the journey, arriving after the bodies were discovered. She would later testify about a ring she had given to her slain brother that Hassell was wearing after his arrest, but she did not testify about her step-father calling her.

George had met Nora at least once before, and the occasion had caused a great deal of tension. Nora and her young husband had come to visit and outfitted Nora's young sister Maudie, who was developing a womanly figure, in Nora's swimsuit. The husband took Maudie into the water tank normally used to water the animals but big enough to use as a swimming pool, and either Susan or George objected to the two frolicking in the water. It caused such a stink that Nora and her husband immediately left and returned to Hemet. There is some family correspondence that indicates Nora may have suspected that George had an unwholesome relationship with Maudie.

Hemet, California is a long way from Farwell, and there is no record of whether these family problems were resolved before the massacre. The long distance between Nora and her mother was likely intentional. Nora's emotions may have still been raw when she got the message to come to Farwell. But she reacted as a daughter should and attempted to contact her mother—who was dead by that time, according to family.

I have no reports of Nora or any of the Fergusons making it to Farwell in time for the mass funeral. But she did appear at the criminal trial, sitting near the front with her relatives. She reportedly refused to look at the defendant.

How Nora settled in Hemet in 1923 is curious because she had no relatives in California at that time. Perhaps her first husband, whose name is lost in time, had a Hemet connection. Hemet is a small farming community in Riverside County at the base of the San Jacinto Mountains. Nora was married five times, possibly as many as three or four times after the murders, and had two daughters.

Her life after the murders was quiet and purposely devoid of any mention of what had happened in Texas. The follow-up stories newspapers print about important cases on various anniversaries never revealed any quotes or contact from Nora. Her obituary following her death on November 19th, 1973 is oddly lacking in personal information—not a hint of her profession or any other details that families usually record for their loved one.

There are obvious reasons why Nora seemed to withdraw after the murders and hunker down in a small town that knew nothing of her family tragedy. For a grieving daughter living with the nightmare of her whole family being slaughtered, Nora very likely sought peace by withdrawing from her Ferguson clan. I could not locate her two daughters or any surviving kin.

Her numerous marriages suggest an inability to connect to others and find somebody who could help her cope with her family tragedy, which she may have suppressed and most certainly kept from the public. She lived her life quietly, shunning any spotlight, avoiding any temptation to satisfy her ego or to correct inaccuracies in the historical record about the massacre.

Nora is buried at San Jacinto Valley Cemetery in Hemet.

A Killer Revealed

Tensions were reaching a fever pitch in the days following the discovery of the bodies of the Hassell family in Farwell. The volatile mood was not fully reported in news accounts and not really understood until Sheriff Martin placed the accused killer in his jail upon his release from the hospital several days after the bodies were discovered.

Court documents show just how quickly authorities had prepared to deal with this family annihilator, who within a few short weeks was condemned to die in the electric chair. Hassell asked for no mercy; no mercy was granted. In fact he was almost lynched by an angry crowd of Texans gathering in town. The mood was so hot that worried sheriffs moved Hassell from the city jail to a nearby town's jail before his trial began.

His Christmas murder spree and attempted suicide made him a national media figure. But who was George Hassell? His life story, documented at the time in news articles and interviews with family and friends, was disappointingly sparse. In late December 1926 and into the first month of 1927, authorities interviewed George Hassell but apparently did little investigation into his motives. Immediately after his arrest, George quickly became a suspect in the death of his older brother, Thomas, but apparently detectives kept confidential any possible new evidence regarding that death and simply concentrated on nailing down the immediate capital murder case. Hassell was interviewed several times by the doctor who treated his self-inflicted wounds; the doctor also considered George's mental well-being, according to the doctor's testimony during the trial.

Any person would wonder how any normal person could murder his entire family, and that question apparently was discussed by attorneys and the judge in preparation for the trial. During the trial, the judge allowed limited witness testimony regarding the state of mind of Hassell in the days surrounding the murder. The record is not clear, but there is no motion or hearing about the possibility of entering an insanity plea.

The law, both in Texas and nationwide, was clear as far back as the mid-1800s on an insanity defense. According to the Texas Criminal Code's Article 47, a defendant is sane if he "intends the natural consequences of his acts." Rarely used as a defense because it is so hard to prove, a defendant can be found not responsible for his crimes after being certified by health officials as insane. The standard of determining whether a defendant was competent to stand trial dates back to thirteenth-century England when "complete madness" was established as a defense and has evolved over the years in England and the U.S. to include judicial decisions laying out guidelines for using the insanity defense. Does the defendant know what is happening, can he help in his defense by cooperating with his attorney, and does he know right from wrong?

Some authorities probably wondered whether Hassell was a madman to have committed such an act. He then was given a series of interviews by the doctor after treating his self-inflicted wounds and looked for any signs of insanity. He then declared him sane.

Though Hassell may have been rational, according to the doctor, it seems to me he was not helping his own defense by continuing to blab to reporters that he deserved what was coming to him for his crimes. Soon after his arrest, Hassell quickly opened up about himself and enjoyed the national limelight. He gave many jailhouse interviews in the days leading up to his trial. His tell-all attitude even continued as he was transferred to state prison. He offered no hint of remorse and seemed a happy-go-lucky guy, although he did say that he expected to pay for his crimes. He was thrilled that his name and deeds were reported in newspapers nationwide and offered to pose for photos. Hassell, once a nobody, was now in the spotlight, perhaps fulfilling a wish to be recognized and noticed.

While Hassell's mental state seemed to satisfy the authorities, his defense attorney pondered what everybody else was wondering: How could any sane person kill his family so viciously? Twice?

The scientific fields of psychology and criminology were fairly new and not fully understood by the residents of Farwell in 1926. People who murdered their families, called family annihilators, were rare at the time—especially in the Texas Panhandle.

While awaiting trial, Hassell became a celebrity figure who loved to chat with the children who flocked to his first-floor prison cell and waited for him to peer out between the bars and begin a conversation. It took several days after his arrest (the attorney who interviewed him testified it occurred "in the latter days" of December) for him to make a full confession about the other murders he had committed in California, and he then seemed upset that the authorities at first doubted his story. He carefully omitted talking about his aliases at first. All the pre-trial publicity confounded his court-appointed attorney, who seemed ready to throw in the towel even before the trial began. What kind of defense can you mount at trial if your client has already confessed to the murders in detail, outraging the community that would eventually judge him?

Any law enforcement officer conducting a murder investigation today would dig into whether the killer might be responsible for other crimes. I suspect that probably didn't happen in 1927, except for the Whittier murders, but only because Hassell admitted to them. Back then it seems likely to me based on my experience covering big news crime stories that police were more likely to avoid any inquiry into something that might embarrass them or call into question their competency, as was the case in Whittier.

Before Hassell was executed, he had made several full confessions to authorities of a life of crime and misadventure, first in Farwell after his arrest and then to the prison warden before his execution. While we know the confessions occurred, most details seem lost to time, and there is some reason to believe Hassell may have embellished or invented some misdeeds.

So what is the true story of George Hassell?

Born July 5th, 1888 in Smithville, Texas, Hassell and his family moved to Oklahoma when he was a toddler. After the death of his mother, he ran away at age fifteen. He later claimed his step-mother killed his father in 1905 by poisoning him and that he abandoned a plot to get a gun and kill his step-mother and her family. He stated that he got too drunk to act on his threat. His step-mother curiously died a short time later from accidentally drinking poison. Where was Hassell at the time?

No one knows. One thing became apparent: His troubles always began with a bout of heavy boozing.

Serious trouble with the law began with his first conviction, for embezzlement, in Abilene, Texas. He was sentenced to two years in prison, probably when he was still a teenager. When he got out, he enlisted in the U.S. Army in Galveston using the alias Stovall, then deserting nine months later while serving at Fort Sam Houston in Texas.

The timeline of Hassell's military career and his first marriage is not clear. According to news reports, he married the first of six women at age eighteen. The bride was Minnie Lofley, whom he pined after for years afterwards, and who bore him a son he only ever heard about and once saw from a distance. Their brief marriage occurred over the strong objections of her family, who may have heard about Hassell's penchant for criminal behavior. After the marriage ended, he enlisted in the U.S. Navy, probably under another alias, and soon deserted in San Francisco. He served three years in federal prison, probably for desertion although I was unable to pin down the exact offense, pining for Minnie and seeking a reconciliation. He reportedly enlisted once again in the U.S. Army and promptly deserted once again. Following his spectacularly failed military career, he traveled to San Angelo, Texas and hooked up with a woman identified as Marie Vogel and her young son. She ran a boarding house. Her past suggests that she may have been a sex worker on the side for extra cash. The couple soon set out for California but ran out of money in Deming, New Mexico. Stranded, they raised $100 by sending Marie to hook up with a man and then threatening to expose him to his family as a deviant. One wonders if the couple used that con on other occasions.

Hassell told reporters he worked in the fields for a while as they headed to California. But this is where the story takes a detour. A former co-worker of mine, Aida Cuevas, who is an archivist and librarian, was curious about my research on Hassell and found a *Sacramento Union* story from 1915 in which Hassell, a woman nicknamed "The Bohemian" (and identified as Marie Vogel), plus a second unidentified man, were being sought by Chicago police for killing a man during a card game. Hassell was identified as the gunman. There is no follow up story and no reports that Hassell was ever arrested or charged with the man's murder. Sometime after that, Hassell and his common-law wife Marie ended up in Whittier, California, where he said he worked in the oil fields. George and Marie adopted two more children, who were brought to them by her mother, then residing in Pittsburgh.

At this point, George and Marie had been a couple for more than seven years. What caused George to suddenly snap and massacre his whole family? According to Hassell's confessions to his prison warden, the day of the murders, George and Marie had argued viciously over George registering for the draft. An enraged George admitted that he then got drunk on whiskey and completely lost his temper, killing first Marie and then the three children: George, eight, an unidentified girl, two, and an unidentified infant. After the murders, he buried the bodies below his cellar by digging out the dirt floor.

After murdering Vogel and the kids, Hassell lived with a Whittier neighbor he reportedly married and then quickly abandoned, according to an unidentified neighbor's report to police.

About eight years passed between the murders in Whittier and Hassell's appearance in Blair, Oklahoma at his brother's widow's home. What was he doing, and where did he go? I could find no documentation in my search for answers, but Hassell shared one hint with a reporter before his execution: He claimed he shipped out as a merchant seaman. After his arrest, an Associated Press story in the *Louisville Courier* in Kentucky reported new details on December 27th, 1926.

Hassell admitted to killing "a woman and three children in California three years ago" (an error in reporting, as the murders were actually about ten years prior). However, he refused at that point to give police names or any details about where this crime occurred. "It was a good job, and nobody will ever know," he told authorities.

The news account continues: "Letters found at his home indicate he worked for the Southern Pacific Railway in California, the Associated Pipe Line Company of Fresno, California, and later the Merchant Marines as a cook on the West Coast. Then he moved to Oklahoma and then moved to a farm near Farwell a year and half ago after marrying his brother's widow."

The events that led him to the doorstep of Aunt Susan are unclear. A series of news stories by the *Amarillo Daily News* reported, without sourcing, that Susan contacted George before he shipped out with the Merchant Marines and reported that Thomas had been killed, asking George to come to Blair and help her harvest the crops. Susan contacted him in New Orleans, but it is unclear if this Merchant Marine stint was an extension of time he already served or a fresh enlistment. The story reports that Hassell came to Blair and finished the harvest, went to Kansas, and then was re-contacted by Susan, who asked him to return. They decided to marry four months after Thomas was killed.

It is easy to assume that George Hassell, a failure his entire life, saw promise for a new life by marrying his brother's widow and becoming associated with the Ferguson clan, a large, extended family with prosperous ranching and farming holdings, from my grandparents' ranch in Colorado to her kin in Oklahoma and Texas.

Author's grandmother, Ethel, seated. Susan Ferguson, far right.

An Odd Couple

How could my great aunt have ever agreed to marry such a charming, conniving man as George Hassell? If she were anything like her younger sister, my grandmother, she would not have put up with a manipulative head case like him. But Hassell seemed to have no problems attracting women with his good looks and big smile, plus his ability to hide his drinking problems, as well as his penchant for violence. In fact he had a certain rugged look and the physique of a man who worked hard in the fields. He also had a jovial personality and enjoyed chatting with people. Children apparently loved him.

I've often wondered how George ended up at the front door of his sister-in-law in Oklahoma. Perhaps George kept in touch with his own family, who gave him the news about the death of his brother Thomas, or maybe he kept in touch with Susan. George certainly needed a place to land for a spell as he moved from place to place, always trying to stay one step ahead of his crimes.

At thirty-nine-years-old, Susan Hassell had been married for twenty-three years, had borne eight children—one married and living in California—and was pregnant when her brother-in-law George showed up. He was thirty-six or thirty-seven and probably extremely solicitous about helping his brother's widow with her farm in Blair as she prepared for the birth of little Sammie.

It's very likely that the marriage of Susan and George was one of convenience. They married several months after the death of Thomas in 1924. Devoutly religious Susan desperately needed help, and George was there to provide the muscle to keep the family from losing the farm that Thomas had worked so hard to keep afloat. But George was not like his brother, who was well-respected and loved by the Ferguson clan.

As most large families used to do, each year the Fergusons gathered at one of the family members' home on a rotating basis for a few days or a week of food and conversation, where kin would share beds, sleep on the floor or porch, or camp out in the yard. A family diary entry from my grandmother shares that George angered the clan with his drinking whiskey and becoming quite obnoxious at one of these events. My mother was ten-years-old at the time of the murders, and my sister believes she met George at the last reunion, probably before they moved to Farwell.

During these years, Prohibition was in effect, although the sale of illicit alcohol was a booming business until Prohibition's repeal in 1933. The Fergusons were devout Free Methodists and thought boozing was sinful and likely were outraged not only by George's illegal drinking but by his terrible behavior when he drank.

The patriarch, Pleasant Ferguson, was a Free Methodist minister, as well as rancher. One wonders how he would have reacted to George making a scene at a good reunion party. Standing six feet, four inches, Pleasant Ferguson by all accounts did not exactly embody his given name.

Pleasant Ferguson's father was a Civil War veteran and received a pension from the Confederacy until he died. Pleasant Ferguson left Tennessee with his family for Texas, where he worked on farms and ranches until marrying Nancy and starting a family.

Great Aunt Susan was one of eleven children of Pleasant and Nancy Ferguson, who settled in Denton, Texas. While Pleasant was tall, Nancy was short and plump—and later became quite round as she aged. According to the family, Nancy was born in Texas in about 1862 and was a midwife of some repute in the area. Susan was the eldest of five daughters, while my grandmother, Ethel, was the youngest, born in 1896.

In 1897 Pleasant and Nancy Ferguson decided to move their family from Denton to the Oklahoma territory near Cordell, where they homesteaded 160 acres. It was dangerous "Indian Country" until Oklahoma became a state in 1907. My grandmother recalled that her parents moved frequently because Pleasant was never content to settle in one spot for long. It's not clear if Pleasant Ferguson actually took part in the stampede of homesteaders, known as "Sooners," who rushed to claim their section of "free land" (that actually had long been the home of the Cherokee Nation).

My grandmother recalled in her diary that she was told by her parents that the family made the long trip from Denton to the Oklahoma territory in a covered wagon in 1897, forging creeks and rivers and moving through the tall grass on the prairie to find the best section of land in one of the earliest moves she can remember. She remembers often walking with her mom and sisters behind the wagon. Pleasant created a home that he dug from the soil and then covered with lumber he hauled by wagon and oxen from a distant town two days away as he framed his family's new home. He planted orchards and grew sorghum that he made into molasses to sell. After a period of farming, Pleasant, who had a sudden urge again to move to greener pastures, sold his profitable farm and moved the family back to the more familiar Texas panhandle outside Perryton in 1910.

Aunt Susan and her husband Thomas Hassell, who came from a Texas ranching family, appeared to have enjoyed a happy marriage. Born Christmas Eve in 1885, Susan married Thomas in Burnett County, Texas on September 4th, 1902, when she was seventeen and Thomas was nineteen. They quickly began raising their big family in Blair, Oklahoma. Thomas died in Oklahoma on July 3rd, 1924. According to one report, Thomas was kicked in the stomach by a mule and died from his injuries. The youngest of his ten children, Samuel, was born seven months after his death. Earlier, in 1910, the couple had lost a sickly one-year-old son. All of the nine remaining children were born in Blair, Oklahoma.

Because Susan was eleven years older than my grandmother, I suspect the two sisters were not particularly close growing up. Grandmother married Forrest Beagle, the son of a prosperous Texas rancher, when she was seventeen in 1913. They immediately started a family. My mother, the second of six children, was born in 1916.

After marrying the widow Susan, George likely felt so uncomfortable with his new Ferguson in-laws that he talked Susan into moving away as far as possible to start a new life. A fiftieth-anniversary four-part series by the *Amarillo Globe News* about the killings that was published in 1976 indicated that the couple fought continuously over the children, and George seemed to feel he was the odd man out in the family. Why they chose to move to Farwell, Texas remained a question for years, until I finally made my own visit to Farwell.

Deadly Details Emerge

Days after George Hassell's arrest, the town of Farwell was becoming a national focal point. Newspapers across the U.S. carried wire stories about Hassell's crime, and each day headlines reported the name "Hassell," the confessed killer of his wife and kids, plus the possibility of a second murdered family in California.

The *El Paso Herald* carried a story December 29th, 1926, stating that Hassell had been spirited away from Farwell's jail in the middle of the night and taken to Hale County jail in Plainview, where he was refusing to answer questions from doctors about his self-inflicted stab wounds to the chest. He was taken on a litter in the back of an automobile to his new cell.

"Crowds had gathered all day Tuesday discussing the crime story related by Hassell, in which he confessed to the killing of his wife and his eight step-children following a quarrel over the oldest girl, Maude, aged fourteen years. He also confessed to killing a woman and three children in California about 1915," the wire story stated.

Newspapers were printing headlines, like the following from the *Zanesville Times Signal* in Ohio:

"Fiend Confesses to Killing His Wife and Eight Children"

Earlier that week, Alabama's *Montgomery Advertiser* reported that "every able-bodied man in the community volunteered in the labors of digging the nine graves." The family was buried side by side, with "the entire citizenship of the community attending the rites."

While the community buried his family, Hassell, still nursing his wounds, was talking to Sheriff Martin and the district attorney about the killings.

Although authorities said they had heard no threat of mob violence, they became extremely concerned by the growing throng of people flocking to the small town, reported *The Eagle* in Bryan, Texas. Police were heavily armed. They were bracing for violence, and it's no wonder authorities decided to act as quickly as possible to bring Hassell to justice. A trial date was set for early January 1927, after a grand jury quickly indicted the farmer on nine counts of murder.

The *Austin American Statesman* set the stage with this headline and story:

Hassell Repudiates Confession

> "Farwell, Texas, Jan. 7—George J. Hassell, facing nine murder charges in connection with the murder of his wife and eight step-children at his farmhouse near this city recently, will plead not guilty when the case is called here today. A change of venue to move to some county other than Parmer will be asked, W. H. Russell, Hereford attorney appointed to represent Hassell, announced. In event the venue change is denied, mitigating pleas will be made.

"Hassell is being heavily guarded and will be brought into court early tomorrow when the selection of a jury is scheduled to begin before Judge Reese Tatum at a special term of the 62nd district court. Every precaution is being taken by Sheriff Martin to prevent any outbreak of reported sentiment and feeling against Hassell.

"Officers from all sections of the Panhandle of Texas will be here. Hundreds of people are arriving, and interest is at high pitch. It is estimated there will be 2,000 people here to hear the trial. Approximately one-third of the special venire of 108 men was empaneled Thursday morning, and the remaining veniremen will be sworn today. The prosecution will be conducted by District Attorney B. N. Richards of Dalhart. Attorney Russell, appointed to defend the prisoner, has been in the law practice at Hereford for many years.

"The first of the nine cases to be tried will be that in connection with the alleged slaying of the oldest boy, Alton Hassell, twenty-one, who, according to Hassell's alleged confession, was shot while asleep. His confession relayed how Hassell described (sic) 'crept up beside him and blew his brains out with a shotgun.'"

Any defense attorney would have had a huge problem with a client like George. He seemed willing to talk to anybody who asked him a question. And his defense attorney would have been worried by the level of prejudicial publicity circulating in town. George Hassell was creating problems for not only himself but also for law enforcement. Sheriff Martin was so worried about the safety of his prisoner that he was moving Hassell from one community jail to another and stepped these moves up to almost daily, depending on the threats received by Sheriff Martin.

Psychopathic behavior can erupt with trigger points, a psychologist friend told me after hearing some of the details of Hassell's murders. But what was the motive?

Early in my research, I hoped the answer might be recorded in the trial transcript that I requested from the Texas Department of Corrections, who found it within the Texas State Archives. The town of Farwell had no public records that dated back that far. It was a long-shot request and quite a surprise when I received word from the archivists that a record did exist.

I discovered what I sought in reading the detail-rich two-inch thick packet of the trial transcript. The motive for this murder spree would be as outrageous in today's violent society as it was in rural Texas back then.

The trial transcript began with the appellate decision by Justice Lattimore on June 15th, 1927 from Austin, denying Hassell's appeal that he was improperly denied a change of venue. The initial motion to move the trial was included, and I looked in vain for any record of where Hassell's attorney, W. H. Russell of nearby Hereford, suggested might be a good alternative town to hold the trial in rather than in Farwell.

The transcript gives a fascinating glimpse into the haste with which the prosecution and District Court Judge Reese Tatum moved the process along over the objections of an appointed counsel, first identified as "Judge" Russell, who tried his best to slow down the fast-moving judicial train and provide the best possible defense for a stubborn client who displayed no interest in taking part in the proceedings. In fact he refused to enter a plea.

Russell was appointed counsel by 69th District Judge Reese Tatum. A veteran judge, Tatum no doubt knew all attorneys who appeared before him. Governor James E. Ferguson appointed Judge Tatum in 1917. Born in Tennessee, the attorney came to Delhart in 1903 and died at age sixty-six in 1940. His obituary does not list his law school background or him presiding over the Hassell case as among his more noteworthy cases.

At age fifty-two, when the trial began, Tatum seems to have taken charge of this case and pushed counsel to move expeditiously to trial. Was he aware or worried about the threat of mob violence? All that would come out after the trial – at least in court filings but not publicly.

On December 29th, Judge Tatum ordered a grand jury to hear the case, and the jury returned nine counts of first-degree murder on January 4th. The next day, the judge ordered jury selection, with the sheriff calling 108 men to face voir dire (or the picking of individual jurors); jurors were to begin hearing the case on Monday, January 7th.

How could the trial proceed in such a small town, where public sentiment ran from hot to boiling? The answer would come in an appellate ruling. It gave a wonderful insight into the public mood prior to trial.

The appellate court ruled that Russell failed to show any proof that Hassell was being denied a fair trial by jurors who had sworn to keep an open mind to all the evidence. All twelve (male) jurors were picked from a pool that represented about half of the qualified jury pool in the county.

The appellate court noted that one juror's statement to Judge Reese during voir dire was very similar in tone to all of the jurors who swore to give Hassell a fair trial. Following is that statement to the court:

"My name is Dud Read, and I live in Lasbuddy in Parmer County. I have lived in Parmer County twelve months and seventeen days. I am from Knox County and have lived in Texas all my life; I am a native of Texas. I am a married man and have two children. I do not know the defendant, George J. Hassell."

PROSECUTOR RICHARDS: "Have you any conscientious scruples with reference to the matter of assessing the death penalty for the crime in the proper case?"

READ: "Yes."

RICHARDS: "You say you have?"

READ: "Oh, no."

RICHARDS: "Well I will ask you. If it developed to be a case that you thought was a proper case for assessing the death penalty, could you assess that penalty?"

READ: "No, sir, I don't believe I could."

RICHARDS: "You don't believe you could. You are opposed to the death sentence?"

READ: "Yes, I sure am."

RICHARDS: "Could you in any case assess the death penalty?"

READ: "Well I guess I could."

RICHARDS: "Well would you?"

READ: "Well according to the evidence."

RICHARDS: "Well then there is a case—there might be a case in which you could assess the death penalty."

READ: "Yes."

RICHARDS: "But if it developed to be what you thought to be a proper case, would your conscience hinder you or prevent you from assessing the death penalty?"

READ: "I don't know."

RICHARDS: "Well there is nobody else that knows."

READ: "No, I am sure of that. According to the evidence."

RICHARDS: "You mean it is just swing to the evidence."

READ: "Yes."

RICHARDS: "Well I take it you mean by that if the case was what you thought was a proper case for it, you could do it so far as your conscience is concerned?"

READ: "Well, no, I don't believe I could."

Judge orders the court to be quiet. "Mr. Richards. I take it he is disqualified. Do you challenge him?"

READ: "All right."

Defense attorney Russell: "Do you mean that?"

READ: "Oh, it could be bad enough that I would give him the death penalty."

RICHARDS: "Well would you do it?"

READ: "Not on circumstantial evidence."

RICHARDS: "I am not asking about that, but if it was a case that you thought justified and required that, would you give it?"

READ: "If it required it, and the evidence told that it did, yes, sir."

The prosecutor continued to press Read for a clear answer on his views, and Read kept vacillating on his answers. Then defense attorney Russell began his voir dire.

RUSSELL: "Have you heard the case discussed?"

READ: "Yes."

RUSSELL: "Read something about it?"

READ: "Yes."

RUSSELL: "Have you heard any talk of mob violence against this defendant?"

READ: "Sure have."

RUSSELL: "Pass the juror back to you."

JUDGE: "Would it take evidence to remove the opinion you have?"

READ: "Do which?"

JUDGE: "Would it take evidence to remove the opinion you have?"

READ: "It would not."

JUDGE: "What do you say, gentlemen?"

RICHARDS: "I would like to ask one more question about that conscientious scrouple (sic) business."

RUSSELL: "We object."

RICHARDS: "All right. The state will accept the juror."

JUDGE: "Stand up and be sworn."

The defense attorney later in his appeal stated that he objected to this juror, and the court incorrectly proceeded and swore him onto the panel. The appellate court disagreed.

Poor Mr. Read seems too confused to answer coherently, and the attorneys and judge elected to not poke him any harder on his sentiments regarding the death penalty in open court, presumably in front of jurors already empaneled or awaiting voir dire. However, it seems strange that the defense attorney failed to be more assertive after opening the door on Mr. Read's comment about mob violence and pre-trial publicity. That would become more apparent after the trial verdict.

However, Justice Lattimore noted in the appeal that the jurors' affidavits stated they had not been affected by any rumors of alleged mob violence. Perhaps the court was satisfied that there was a lot of talk in town but nothing to merit moving the trial elsewhere.

The ruling included a quote from a prospective juror's affidavit that stated the juror, if chosen to hear the trial, could disregard those news stories and the potential of mob violence and could impartially hear the evidence.

Justice Lattimore quoted from the affidavit made to the court during the jury selection or voir dire, "I have merely formed an impression as to his guilt from what I read and heard, but if I were selected as a juror, I could wholly disregard what I may have heard or read about the matter, not take that into consideration but try the case and decide the case solely from the testimony produced on the witness stand. And I would do that."

The statement is clearly written in terse, precise, and impartial legal language. It is doubtful that any prospective juror could have written such an articulate statement without an attorney's assistance. Moreover the appellate ruling noted that most of the other jurors' affidavits contained similar language. Writing such an affidavit no doubt came as a result of a hastily scheduled pre-trial hearing where the prosecution and defense dealt with the incredibly tough issue of finding a jury panel to hear this case, reporting on which bordered on sensationalism.

Where else could Parmer County, a sparsely populated expanse of farm and ranch land, have afforded to move a trial judge and his staff plus a heavily guarded prisoner? The expense would have been enormous, even in those days. Judge Tatum might have had to consider moving the trial hundreds of miles away from Farwell if he had found sufficient evidence that Hassell could not get a fair trial locally.

Most adult men in the 1920s were fortunate enough to have had sufficient schooling to read, write, and keep track of what money they made. If they graduated from high school or college, they likely were pillars of the community. Farwell, as a ranching and farming town, provided Hassell a jury comprised of his peers.

It can be assumed that Judge Tatum and attorneys were eyeing prospective jurors for men who had common sense and would understand the testimony they were about to hear. In effect they didn't want any silly arguments erupting about Hassell's constitutional rights being violated as jurors were being selected.

In the appeal, Justice Lattimore concluded, "The attorney appointed by the court to represent the appellant appears to have performed the disagreeable duty with commendable zeal and ability. From the record, it appears that the trial was orderly and deliberate and no prejudicial effort has been perceived."

In 1926 court reporters performed an extremely important court function, just as they do today. But back then the court reporter had a tedious job. Stenographers took notes by shorthand and then spent hours, if not days, transcribing the proceedings into a typed transcript, tapping out reams of testimony.

Defense counsel had a particularly tough time with insufficient time to review testimony, prepare motions, or even prepare much of a defense. Counsel probably had to rely on his own good notes and memory. A day's worth of typed trial transcript from the reporter was highly unlikely.

In small towns, residents rallied around families stricken by grief. The Ferguson family did not get to Farwell in time for the funerals, I later learned from the transcript. But whenever they did arrive, the Fergusons expected answers from the preliminary investigation.

An angry community, embarrassed by the unwanted publicity of a mass murderer living among them, was anxious to put closure to the case. George Hassell had confessed in jail. Why delay meting out justice, residents probably were thinking.

From news stories of the day, it is clear that crowds of men and women were gathering in town to find out anything they could about the murders, and I was curious where they would have stayed or camped. Farwell probably had insufficient rooms or hotels to accommodate several thousand visitors. And the courthouse, I assumed, would have had trouble dealing with the throng and the uptick in security.

The murders began on or about December 2nd, 1926; Hassell's trial started January 10th. Word of the trial must have taken several days to transmit, and it appears that few journalists covered the trial as thoroughly as today's journalists would. The news reports appeared to be written from interviews of court officials attending the trial.

News coverage of criminal trials was not a guarantee in 1926, and Judge Tatum may have decided to bar the press from the courtroom to put the lid on flaring tempers in the community. Very few details about the trial were reported in news clips that I uncovered. The accounts covered the basics: Who, what, where.

The publisher of the Clovis, New Mexico, daily newspaper told me that the trial and crime *were* covered thoroughly back then. Unfortunately most of those detailed stories of the trial have been lost to time.

Imagine a heinous murder in a small town where most people are not well read nor well educated. If there were a town newspaper, readership probably was pretty limited. Neighbors shared newspapers. Telephones were a luxury. Telegraph often was the quickest form of communication. However, nothing could have beaten the rumor mill and gossip among Farwell residents, and the atmosphere had to be rageful as the throng waited outside the courthouse for any scrap of news.

There was still no clear image of George Hassell in any news clipping, and I could not track down a mug shot from police files or the archives until much later in my research.

Hassell was joking and talking to his jailers, and they, in turn, probably were discussing the case among themselves. Word must have reached the community that George Hassell was not showing much remorse over the killings.

The transcript, although fascinating to read, could not fully convey what was occurring inside the courthouse. I tried to imagine the scene as I read the words about a man I came to despise and a great aunt about whom I was beginning to form a mental picture.

George J. Hassell v. State of Texas

As the trial began, the court spent considerable time laying the foundation for introducing George Hassell's confession into evidence. In the haste to get the trial under way, it seems few had even read the confession—not even the defendant. The trial transcript reveals some surprising legal steps.

The session began when defense attorney Russell moved to order the prosecution to choose which murder charge it would use in the trial: Susan Hassell or which one of the eight children.

JUDGE TATUM: "Over-ruled."

RUSSELL: "Note our exception."

It is unclear which count the prosecution would introduce first until testimony started to focus on the last victim, eldest son Aldon.

The prosecution then called its first witness, and it appears the use of Hassell's confession was the key to the prosecution's case. The opening testimony seems to serve as more of what in today's court proceedings would be called a preliminary hearing, where all the legal maneuvering is hashed out before the actual trial begins. Normally a preliminary hearing lays out the evidence and allows the judge to rule on which of the charges have sufficient evidence to proceed to trial.

"My name is J. D. Thomas, and I occupy the official position of County Attorney for the Parmer County, Texas and held that position during November and December 1926.

"I know the defendant, George J. Hassell. He made a statement to me, along the latter days of December 1926, with reference to the offense for which he is on trial. That statement was made out in the jail, and I believe Sheriff Martin, Sheriff Kennedy of Clovis, and Mr. W. H. Holmes, and possibly Jake McLain, were present together with myself. Mr. Hassell dictated his statement to the stenographer.

RICHARDS: "I will ask you, Mr. Thomas, whether or not previous to his making that statement, you, as County Attorney, warned the defendant that he did not have to make any statement."

THOMAS: "I did."

RUSSELL: "We object to that. The statement must contain that information if it is there."

JUDGE TATUM: "I will over-rule that."

RUSSELL: "Note our exception."

THOMAS: "I said I did warn him that he did not have to make any statement whatever, and I further warned him if he should make any statement the same might be used in evidence against him."

RUSSELL: "My objection goes to that. That should be contained in the written statement."

JUDGE: "I think you should have to lay a predicate. I presume that is his objection. I will give you a bill on that."

RUSSELL: "All right."

THOMAS: "After I had warned him in that manner, he made his statement in his own words. I had previously arranged for the Court stenographer to be there. Mr. Hassell communicated his desire to make a confession through Sheriff

Martin, and I had arranged for the Court Reporter, Mr. Holmes at Clovis, to be present at the time. And Mr. Hassell dictated his statement, and as he dictated it, the reporter took it down in shorthand.

That statement was made in narrative form, and as he dictated it, the stenographer took it down in shorthand."

RICHARDS: "I will ask you, Mr. Thomas, whether or not the statement was apparently made voluntarily?"

RUSSELL: "We object to that."

JUDGE: "Over-ruled."

RUSSELL: "Note our exception."

THOMAS: "As far as I could tell, it was made voluntarily. Afterwards the stenographer returned with the statement transcribed on the typewriter, and I was present when he returned with it. The defendant then signed the statement.

You hand me what will be state's Exhibit Number One and ask me to look at that and see whether or not that is the statement about which I have been testifying, and in reply, I will say that it is; that is the statement that the defendant signed at that time, and I attested it there as a witness who saw him sign it."

CROSS-EXAMINATION

RUSSELL: "Was the written instrument you identified read over to the defendant before he signed it?"

THOMAS: "No, sir, it wasn't. We asked if he wanted . . ."

RUSSELL: (interrupting) "I didn't ask you that. Did he read it himself? Your honor, we object because the confession is a thing which was never read to the defendant, and he never read it but signed something. Unless you can lay the proper predicate by going further . . ."

RICHARDS: "We haven't got through yet."

JUDGE: "Well I will over-rule it."

RUSSELL: "That will be all at this time."

RE-DIRECT EXAMINATION BY RICHARDS

"When the stenographer returned with the statement that was transcribed, I asked Mr. Hassell if he wanted it read, and if he did, that I would read it, and he said he preferred not, if it was just like he dictated it; and with that explanation, he signed it. He had a full and free opportunity to read it; I made that clear to him and even volunteered to read it two or three times, and he said he preferred not to read it on account of his feeling."

RE-CROSS BY MR. RUSSELL:

"You ask me if he was under arrest and in jail all that time. I presume so; he was in the custody of the Sheriff."

WITNESS EXCUSED

The prosecution then called the stenographer, William W. Holmes of Clovis, New Mexico, who testified about the process of taking the confession in shorthand and then transcribing it, and explaining that he did not compare his transcribed document to his notes. He also remembered Hassell declining to read it.

Defense attorney Russell then re-called County Attorney Thomas to the witness stand.

RUSSELL: "Mr. Thomas, at the time Mr. Hassell made this alleged confession and dictated it to the Court Reporter, Mr. Holmes, and especially at the time you carried it back to Mr. Hassell at the jail after it had been transcribed."

RICHARDS: "The State will now offer in evidence as Exhibit Number One the written statement and confession made by the defendant, which has been identified by two witnesses."

RUSSELL: "I would like to ask Mr. Thomas one more question."

RICHARDS: (To Mr. Thomas) "Take the stand."

"Mr. Thomas, at the time Mr. Hassell made this alleged confession and dictated it to the Court Reporter, Mr. Holmes, and especially at the time you carried it back to Mr. Hassell at the jail after it had been transcribed by Mr. Holmes, there was considerable talk of mob violence at that time, wasn't there?"

THOMAS. "Well I don't know that I can say there was. I have heard of mob violence, but I never have known of any mob violence around here coming from any authentic source. I have heard rumors (sic) here and there, but I couldn't tell you whether or not it came from here or anything about it."

RICHARDS: "Also, isn't this a fact that Mr. Martin, the Sheriff of this County, told Hassell he wouldn't take time to read it because he was afraid a mob might form and he was.

THOMAS (interrupting): "I never heard the Sheriff make a remark like that." (Witness excused)

RUSSELL: "Now we will object to the confession as a whole for the reason the proper predicate hasn't been laid. It is not shown that this was a free and voluntary statement of this defendant or that he was made known of its contents before he signed it; and we will make the further objection, general objection, that if the confession or alleged confession is admitted in evidence at all, we object to any part of it being admitted, except that with reference to the particular transaction or homicide that we are on trial about. I haven't read the whole instrument, but I do understand that this confession contains a lot of other matters about various other things."

JUDGE TATUM: "I don't think that part, except matters contemporaneous with this matter would be admissible. Of course I don't know whether there are any in there or anything about it. (pause) I will over-rule it for the present time."

RICHARDS: "Gentlemen, I will read it to you."

Speedy Justice

What a way to open this murder trial. Get to the point as fast as possible and then let's all go home seemed to be the attitude the prosecution displayed as the trial offered up several witnesses testifying about Hassell dictating his confession.

But the court papers lacked the color that I had hoped to find. It did not contain the opening statements because the appellate court, which filed the transcript, does not consider opening statements as evidence. They are considered "road maps" to guide jurors through the evidence. The transcript of opening statements is lost.

I wanted to know what the courtroom looked like. Did Hassell wear prison garb, or was he wearing his old bib overalls or maybe the suit of his dead brother? How many deputies were assigned to the courtroom? Was it noisy? Was the Farwell courtroom large enough for this proceeding? Where were the defendant and his attorney sitting? Was Hassell chained and shackled?

Indeed the transcript almost appears to be sanitized of any wrangling over the confession. From the transcript, the trial was conducted in an extremely civil manner. The court reporter, however, failed to record some of the questions asked by attorneys, instead paraphrasing and incorporating the question in the witness' answer. Punctuation and some answers are a bit confusing.

In January 1927, George Hassell was made aware of his rights, was provided an attorney, and was convicted without apparent prejudice, according to the appellate justice's opinion.

Sure, Hassell made a statement after his arrest, but he chose to do so despite being warned of his constitutional rights regarding self-incrimination. The transcript, made many years before Miranda rules and subsequent rulings about police interrogations, reveals that attorneys spent some time assuring the court and jurors that Hassell was well aware of his constitutional rights and was of sound mind to make a decision about whether to talk to authorities. He was not insane at the time of his arrest or trial, the court ruled.

Today defendants in capital cases awaiting execution are granted different attorneys specializing in appeals and attempting to point out the weaknesses of the defendant's trial attorney, hoping to overturn a conviction because of incompetent counsel. Attorney Russell, probably one of a small handful of qualified defense attorneys in the region, handled the appeal himself. It is difficult to assess whether Russell was up to the task or whether he had sufficient time to analyze the trial and ponder his best strategy. His challenge was almost impossible, considering the pace of the proceedings and the speed with which the state of Texas wanted to carry out the death penalty after all appeals were denied.

Convincing a jury to acquit Hassell, it would seem, nowadays, was out of the question. Portraying Hassell as a strange man who suddenly went berserk might have been his best strategy. However, it seems Russell really had little time to mount a decent defense, and Hassell was an unpopular man whose own family—or those who could be located—seemed unwilling to come to his defense.

Consider this poor defense attorney in this town as the trial began. He must have been an honorable and trusted officer of the court in order to be appointed to represent this accused killer in such a high stakes case. Consider Atticus Finch in Harper Lee's classic *To Kill a Mockingbird.* Russell was in a similar unenviable position. As an attorney, he had an obligation to obey the law and provide the best counsel he could for his client. Russell had to represent his client, but also not upset the judge with delays. Moreover he had to live and work in this area after the trial concluded, and that meant he could not afford to antagonize the town or jurors by making this a case about a man who was innocent.

Russell may have been subjected to rude remarks or even hateful ones for representing Hassell. He undoubtedly was under a great deal of pressure. His job was to provide legal counsel. He didn't have to like his client. But I wondered if he was pressured to take short cuts in order for this trial to proceed so expeditiously. If so I could not tell from reading the transcripts.

I would discover much later in reading Texas journalist and author Lana Payne Barnett's book, *Lonely Graves*, a wonderful account of three notorious murders in Texas that after Russell wrapped up the trial, he told the judge that he no longer wanted to see the defendant. His client disgusted him, and Russell left town after the jury began deliberations, which later caused a major legal problem for the court. Because his attorney left the court before the verdict was read, and the attorney neglected to immediately file Hassell's appeal before the sentencing, Governor Dan Moody would later delay the execution as an appeal was eventually filed, Barnett wrote in her description of the case. The people of Farwell collected $113 for Russell, who was never compensated by the state for his services, writer Barnett discovered.

With that insight, it is fascinating to speculate about the relationship between Hassell and his attorney. In capital murder cases nowadays, attorneys and clients are thrown into a close working relationship that often spans years before the case goes to trial. If the defendant doesn't like his attorney, he can fire him and request another and occasionally even seek permission from the court to represent himself.

On the other side of the attorney's table was the prosecutor. His job was much easier.

Mr. B. N. Richards represented the state of Texas as the prosecutor. The prosecutor who was initially involved in the Hassell murder investigation as he prepared for trial stepped aside. County attorney J. D. Thomas, who took Hassell's confession and probably played a huge role, along with the sheriff, in preparing the case, probably was not as skilled a criminal trial attorney as Richards, who did all the questioning for the prosecution.

On the bench was Judge Tatum, who was presiding over the biggest case of his career. He surely was aware that appellate justices would later review his actions on the bench, parsing every motion and decision for errors.

Although not included in the transcript, the judge probably followed procedure with a pleasant greeting to jurors on such a solemn occasion and an admonition to follow the evidence and put aside any personal conclusions until the case was concluded. The opening statements would be filled with promises from the prosecutor to produce evidence that would show Hassell was a killer and a plea from his defense attorney to listen carefully for signs of an unstable man. But the actual record was blunt and devoid of color. Jurors, all men, were read the indictment, which only included a single count of capital murder of Aunt Susie's son, Aldon, by gunshot on December 6th.

Judge Tatum then arraigned Mr. Hassell.

"What do you plead at this time, Mr. Hassell?"

Hassell: "I refuse to plead."

"The court will enter a plea of not guilty for the defendant. You may be seated."

The pleading was curious. Was this trial whizzing along so fast that Hassell had not yet been arraigned? Perhaps this was a redundant pleading from an earlier hearing for which there is no known record.

Judged by His Peers

The drama in the courtroom must have been spellbinding. The attorneys and judge were primed and ready, anxious to display their skill and commitment to justice. Was Hassell nervous? Was there a lot of noise of shifting chairs and clearing of throats as everybody sat down to hear the confession? Was it cold in the courtroom in January? What was the weather like outside for the hundreds waiting there? That time of the year, the winds can blow with a fury that topples what few trees there are on the flat prairie, and tumbleweeds the size of pianos roll along in herds, getting caught up in the barbed wire fencing.

I was disappointed to find the transcript missing comments by the prosecutor or Hassell's attorney and often missing the questions they asked each witness. Today a trial transcript contains every word spoken while court is in session. Even when the jury is excused while attorneys hash out legal arguments and the judge makes evidentiary rulings, the court reporter writes every single word.

Judge Tatum could have asked the defendant if he were comfortable or had eaten prior to the early start. Hassell had an appetite. Was he shackled? The judge might want those removed out of sight of the jury panel. He may have asked the men in the jury if they wanted to write notes on the evidence or if they could adequately hear the officers of the court. Did he admonish the spectators in the court to keep quiet? And I wondered if any newspaper journalist was present and if the judge admonished the jury not to read any news accounts of the proceeding.

Sometimes defense attorneys in such cases choose to make their opening statement when they begin their defense instead of at the beginning of the trial. They may choose to let the passions subside before opening their case with words of caution to jurors not to prematurely judge Hassell before hearing all the evidence. Sadly there was no documentation revealing Russell's strategy for dealing with the damning confession his client had made.

I tried to conjure up an image of the courtroom. Was it an ornate wood-paneled room flanked with the flags of the United States and the state of Texas, or was it a public room converted for the purpose of this particular trial? How many people were in attendance? Was the black-robed judge, Judge Reese Tatum, elevated above the courtroom, sitting behind the proverbial bench that proclaims his authority as master of the courtroom? Were the defendant, defense attorney, and two prosecutors placed at desks behind the bar that separates the public from the officers of the court?

I wondered if the courtroom was heated from a wood burning stove or a noisy oil furnace. The trial was heard in the dead of winter, and outside temperatures were hovering around freezing. Any spectator who ventured outside to smoke or confer with those outside the courtroom probably lost his coveted seat.

The setting of the trial was of keen interest to me, and I dreamed of a trek to Farwell to see for myself what this venue looked like so long ago.

The few news stories of that day stated that Susan Hassell's family was in attendance. Susan's father and brother were named—but not my grandmother, who was residing in Pueblo, Colorado at the time. Perhaps Grandmother chose not to attend because of the horrendous circumstances. I was again saddened that I never had a chance to ask her about that event. I tend to think she and my mom were shielded from the ugly facts about the case.

I read these passages and thought about how this would play in a modern courtroom. In capital cases, attorneys and the judge spend numerous days hammering out legal issues pertaining to the admissibility of evidence. In this case, the testimony about the confession only lasted a few minutes. In today's proceedings, one or more hearings would involve testimony from police about how the confession was made. The defense attorney would want to know whether Hassell was thinking properly about his rights before he began confessing. Without the aid of a tape recorder, a defense attorney might question how the confession was transcribed and whether it was accurate. In today's pre-trial hearings, every person who was present would be interviewed about what they heard or saw.

In today's judicial proceedings, this trial could be appealed under assertions that it was nothing but a rush job, with Hassell not being given adequate legal counsel before he began talking to police.

And now Hassell was sitting in a courtroom and about to hear his words describing what he did. I thought about how he might be reacting to this dramatic moment.

Was Hassell watching the jurors? I'm quite sure jurors were watching this man for any telltale sign of remorse. They would want all the questions that had been raised about the murders answered one by one. I have served as a juror on two criminal trials, one involving a serial child molester and another involving a man who carjacked a young woman and was about to kill her in the desert when she tumbled out of the car to safety. All of us jurors watched the defendant very closely and later remarked about his demeanor as we pondered his fate in the jury room.

Defense attorneys warn their clients that jurors are paying rapt attention to them at every moment, but I always felt as though I could read innocence or guilt on defendants' faces when victims testified. How would Hassell look as his statement was read?

The Confession

"My name is George Jefferson Hassell. I was born at Smithville, Texas, July 26th, 1888 and moved to Oklahoma in 1898, I guess it was. My mother died in 1901. I ran away from home in November of that year. My father died in 1905, I believe it was, but I wouldn't be sure. He was poisoned by my step-mother. That was my first impulse to commit a crime. I went out to the place to kill the whole bunch of them, but I got too much whiskey and didn't use any gun. That was my first impulse to commit a crime. You ask me how old I was at the time. Well I must have been somewhere in the neighborhood of fifteen years. I forget the exact dates."

Actually, when his father died, he would have been seventeen-years-old. I doubt jurors had time to consider that math discrepancy because the confession was chock full of other vital information for them to consider. They were probably sitting in rapt silence. This was what they were chosen to hear. They had sworn to hear all the evidence and return a verdict based on facts, not emotion. But the emotion inside the courtroom certainly did not escape these jurors who probably felt this job one of the most serious civic obligations they ever accepted.

The confession continued.

"My father died in Texas close to Fort Worth, and my mother died in Oklahoma. Shortly following my father's death—I must have been older than fifteen—but shortly following his death, I got in with bad company in Abilene, drinking whiskey and embezzeled some money, for which I served a term of two years in the Texas State Penitentiary."

RUSSELL: "All of that is objected to."

JUDGE: "Gentlemen, you will not consider that part as evidence."

RUSSELL: "The whole thing is getting in. We object to it going in and ask that it be withdrawn from the jury."

JUDGE: "I can't take time to look it over myself. You will have to."

RUSSELL: "We will have to take the instrument and have the time off to do it."

JUDGE: "All right. I will give you the time to check it."

In the haste to get the trial underway, I was amazed neither attorney Russell nor the judge had time to read the entire confession to determine if there were any statements that could be deemed inadmissible. It's unknown how long it took, but the court reconvened with Russell addressing the judge.

Today capital murder trials spend months in pre-trial meetings and in-court sessions discussing issues, such as any confession. I have covered pre-trial hearings where the judge and attorneys tediously hash out a transcript of a taped confession line by line over many hours.

Judge Tatum presumably ordered the trial to resume after reaching an agreement out of the presence of the jury and probably spectators.

RUSSELL: "We are objecting to all the contents of this instrument, of course, as I stated in the beginning. Now we are objecting to all of it save and except the last paragraph on page

11, indicated by a check mark in pencil and down to about the middle of page 12, which is indicated by a cross mark, for the reasons stated a while ago—because it is with reference to different matters entirely foreign to any matters connected with the particular homicide in question. Those are the parts we are objecting to for the reasons stated. All the balance of it we are objecting to."

JUDGE: "Down to Page 7 where I marked on the left-hand margin X you will omit. From page 1 down to 7, down to where it is marked X on the left-hand margin, I will sustain. The other I will admit."

RUSSELL: "Note our exception."

Today the confession would be redacted before the trial after the judge, prosecutor, and defense attorney hashed out all the legal arguments even before a jury was seated. Although jurors are instructed not to consider the objectionable statement, it's obvious this point would be in any juror's mind and not easily forgotten. At that moment, jurors probably were wondering about the intervening years of Hassell's life. A juvenile offender probably would not be sent to an adult prison. A first offense likely would not result in a two-year sentence, unless there were extenuating circumstances involving other incidents. But prosecutors had no choice but to accept Hassell's sworn confession that he had a prison record in Texas.

The jury was not supposed to consider anything about Hassell's past. The confession continued.

"... And last fall, a year ago, we had quite a settee down picking cotton, which worked an unjust cause. I started to pack up and leave and did pack up to leave but didn't use judgment enough to leave, but that is the thing I ought to have done, ought to have walked out. Anyhow spats began to come in frequent. She (Susan) would always uphold her children on any correction I would make and fusses come more frequent and plentiful."

What was this all about? George and Susan were fighting over some issue. He was going to leave her, he said.

"We had the daughter in California and her husband to come to our place last summer. She was with another man she had married. She had married again. There was something I was about to tell that wouldn't amount to a thing in the world, and I believe I will just leave it out.

"It may just caused a separation between daughter and her husband as it came pretty near causing one when they were here. Well maybe I had better put it in order to get this straight. She had a bathing suit on this other girl, the one that was home, put this bathing suit on and she got in a wooden tank out there at my place bathing. She couldn't swim, and his wife went on back in the house and come out again in a few minutes, and he had his hand in a suspicious place, and she got mad and was going to sue him for a divorce, and that night or the night after that, they were leaving in a couple few days, she told the girls' (sic) mother about it so the girls' mother got after her and was telling me about it, and the girls' mother accused me of doing the same thing, and she said she thought the girl was in a family way then and she was going to take her to Clovis to a doctor to see whether she was or wasn't, and I told her that was a good idea, that I would do with her and so—for some reason I didn't go, but one of the boys went with her."

Was Hassell's motive for murder becoming clearer?

"She taken the boy to an osteopath down at Clovis, but she didn't tell him, just told him—No, that was a month later than that or more—it was in August she taken the girl, but we made a trip up in Colorado in July."

My grandparents' farm was in Pueblo, Colorado. A great uncle had a ranch nearby. This must have been the time my mother told my sister that she suspected Maudie was being raped by Hassell.

"It was in August she taken the girl to the doctor. Just because of her missing a period, he gave her a treatment, and for a while my wife talked to me all the time about this girl being in a family way, and I tried to reason with her and tried to tell her things like that had happened, and if it had, we would have to take care of her. Three times, I think, she went to this doctor around the time the period was supposed to be. It was plain enough to see that she was in a family way all right. So I had been aiming to go to the oil fields when we got our crop gathered up to get enough money to start another crop on, and of course I believe my wife thought my idea of going to the oil fields was to get a chance to hike off, which if she would have let me go to the oil fields no doubt, but what I would never have come back – I would probably have kept on going, and she fussed around about me going to the oil fields and she said if I went that she was going too and so forth, so any how we had a fuss this night and we laid there and fussed I guess until twelve o'clock, and I got up and dressed and went out and sat in the other room, and she gets up and comes in there and tells me to come back to bed. I had a pint of whiskey in the barn and I went down to the barn and got me a drink of this whiskey and I went back and started to lay down, and she smelled this whiskey, and it roused her again."

In his confession, Hassell was artfully avoiding any direct admission that he had raped his niece, who was also his stepdaughter. Domestic spats between married couples can involve a lot of shouting, throwing objects, cursing, and maybe some violent shoving or punching. Although it is not clear, Susan apparently was only giving him the silent treatment.

As any mother would act, Aunt Susan would want to protect her daughter and her family. There could be no suitable explanation from George Hassell. Was Aunt Susan preparing to call Sheriff Martin in the morning? Had she thrown out this vile man she had apparently married out of convenience? Had he been told to leave and never come back? The confession gives no hint, and Hassell probably was like any killer trying to put the best spin on an awful deed. He wanted to go; she wanted him to stay and was even willing to follow him to the oilfields, he said. This was hard to believe in context of what happened next.

"Now I am honest—I don't know how come the hammer [got] there. I never put it there and didn't know it was in the house, but that was the first thing I seen—was the hammer, a ballpeen hammer. . .and hit her twice before I could stop myself and then I shut her wind off with my hand to keep the sound in and then all blood commenced running everywhere, and I thought I had her passed (sic) any noise and I kinda let up on her wind pipe, and she began making a noise, and I taken a stocking and tied it around her throat to stop the noise, and about the time I had that done, that the little fellow was laying there and he commenced to hollering and putting up a noise, and I just reached over and choked him."

A ball peen hammer in the bedroom is unusual, even for a rural farmhouse. Some people keep revolvers handy for protection. If this testimony were true, one explanation could be that Susan retrieved the hammer from the barn and kept it near her for protection against Hassell. Ironically I learned from my sister, Kathy, that our grandmother kept a hammer at her bedside when she rented upstairs bedrooms to boarders after our grandfather's Parkinson disease worsened and immobilized him. Did Grandmother take a hint from her elder sister Susan about keeping a hammer handy?

It's easier to think Hassell was lying about the hammer when he confessed and was trying to portray himself as being impulsive instead of conniving, out of his mind in rage rather than a scheming killer.

Aunt Susan and little Sammie apparently were sleeping side by side in the bed. This thirty-nine-year-old man, who was described as "burly," was somebody who had labored in the oilfields and farm fields his entire life. He no doubt was strong. Choking a woman and her children would not be hard for such a man. And as the world would later learn, he had experience in choking people.

Hassell had succeeded in not awakening the rest of his family. Hard-working people in need of sleep tend to ignore noises until they become too loud to ignore. The other children continued to sleep. Hassell expressed some remorse at that point in his confession.

Hassell turned his full attention to the crying baby.

"I choked him with my hand and then tied the stocking on after—he wasn't hit at all. None of the little ones were hit. So I had started and Lord-God (sic) I would have given anything in the world if I had not made the first lick, but I had started it and I finished it."

There were more children to kill. There could be no witnesses. This quote stands out as the most telling comment I discovered in the transcript. If I were a headline writer, this would be the one to top the page 1 story of George Hassell's confession.

" . . . But I had started it and I finished it."

He went to another bedroom to choke to death two other young children, David, seven, and Johnnie, six, then used the hammer to kill the pregnant step-daughter whose condition set off this whole bloody spree. Two older boys would be killed next. Virgel, thirteen, and Russell, nine, who had been sleeping, began fighting off Hassell as he attacked them. Virgel was the strongest and scratched and punched Hassell on the face and hands. But the much stronger Hassell broke free and grabbed a shotgun. He killed Virgel with a blast to the heart and then stalked Russell, who was hiding from the rampaging Hassell.

"I am not trying to whip the devil around the stump and I am not trying to get any sympathy because I don't deserve any sympathy, but after I go to these three little ones choked, I taken a hammer—the same hammer—and went into the daughter's room and hit her twice and then finished by choking her. The oldest boy, being away working with the thresher, Virgil (sic) and Russell was sleeping in the back room, so I goes back and wakes Russell up and tell him to go get in his bed. Virgil wakes up and says, 'Did Alvin (probably meant Aldon) come home?' and I said 'No.' And Russell grabs his clothes and goes on and gets in his bed, and I built a fire, but Virgil after that didn't go back to sleep, and I just goes in there and starts choking Russell. He was the only one I hit with the axe, and he began to make a noise; I couldn't handle him the way I had the rest of them, so Virgil come in there and kinda got his bearing and says, 'Daddy, what in the world are you doing, trying to kill somebody?' And I say, 'Get out of here and attend to your business,' and he grabbed at me. Of course I had to let this other fellow go, and in the meantime though, I was afraid, so I taken the shotgun from where it was and put it in another place, and at least one of the boys said, 'Get the shotgun' and called 'Mamma' for a little while then or called 'Maudie,' that was the girl, and while this other boy and myself was on the floor fighting – he was a kind of a chunk of a boy – Virgil hollered for Russell to come and help him, that he would get the son-of-a-bitch, and Russell he picked up a brick and hit me two or three times with a brick, but of course that don't justify me, but I am just telling the straight of it—so after I seen I was going to have a pretty tussle with both of them and after they had scratched me up here and bungled me up, I just swung loose from them and jumped up and run into the room and grabbed the shotgun, and when Virgil walked into the room the other way, I shot him right through the heart, and of course he fell there in the dining room; that was in the dining room where I shot him and where the stove was. So Russell he did—guess he got scared and opened the door and run back into the boys room and got in the corner of the closet, and so I hunted for him, and when I found him, I got down on the floor and choked him. Just got him down on the floor and choked him, choked him with my hand and then I tied – I don't know what I tied around his neck, but I tied something to stop that noise. After it was all through, I goes and gets Virgil first; he was in the dining room, and I think I rolled him over on a quilt and dragged him out to the cellar and I believe he was lying next to the wall on the west side. Russell was laying at the north end. I got Russell next, and he kept wheezing—like this—(illustrating), something like that, and I was afraid it sounded awful loud; it sounded awful loud to me, and I was afraid somebody might be passing and would hear it to the road, and so I gets this axe and hits him, and that was the only one I hit with the axe. After I choked him and he wouldn't stop wheezing, I hit him."

This point is curious. Only one of the nine was killed with an axe. In Hassell's mind, that somehow made his actions less heinous. He was rationalizing his despicable behavior. Surely he thought the authorities would understand.

Hassell still was not finished killing.

The eldest Hassell son, Aldon, was working in Clovis threshing wheat for extra family income and was not due home for another four days (Aldon's name was misspelled as Alton in countless news clippings). Hassell could have bolted from the bloody scene and disappeared in the dark for the oilfields—and nobody would have discovered the bodies until Aldon came home.

"Now mind you there was another one that wasn't there that I hadn't got out of the way, and that was the oldest boy. This was on Wednesday—about Wednesday. He was to come home from the thresher on a Saturday night, but he didn't come home Saturday. I sat up until about midnight for him. Sunday evening at sundown, he came in. That was the Sunday it sleeted and rained."

If there were any sympathy for Hassell and his plight, what happened next would erase that emotion. Hassell was a conniving and brutal killer plotting his next move.

"So we had supper, killed a chicken, and went and drove the chickens up and got the ducks up off the pond and sat around there and played cards until after midnight, and I told him the folks had gone to see Aunt Liddy (one of Susan's sisters) down at Shallowater, that is where I made up that story at. Well I knowed I had to do something; I had some more whiskey on hand. In the meantime—I think it was four o'clock the next morning, I got up and took me a drink of whiskey to help my nerve and I went to the side of his bed with the shot gun and shot him right through there somewhere (indicating head). Yes, that was while he was asleep, and he never did know anything about it. He never knowed anything about it and died easier than any of them, and I put him on the other side of the dugout and began covering the dirt in from the other side. Yes, I put the bedding in with him, but the others I kept the bedding covered up until I could burn them, but the bedding he was on, I just put it in there. I didn't know what to do and I was just like a mad man or a crazy man, I don't know what. But anyhow I done what I did and I am here to pay my penalty like a man, whatever it may be. I tried my best to make it a death penalty; I tried to stab myself. I tried to find my heart, but I couldn't do it, and after this attempt I made to commit suicide, I had Lendolph (meaning Lindop) come in and get the sheriff himself and bring him out and I said, 'Here is what they tried to do to me.' That is what I thought I said and then I showed the knife."

His confession probably took some time to read. It was jumbled, but it sounded like the George Hassell some of the townsfolk knew. A simple man, but somebody whose words are frighteningly real and carried such weight, even as the prosecutor read them.

He had just described killing nine people. But authorities apparently asked him some questions pertinent to the girl Maudie.

"You ask me if I actually had sexual intercourse with the girl that was in a family way, and to answer to your question, I will say 'Yes, I had sexual intercourse with the girl.' You ask what I intended doing. Well I told my wife, as soon as we found out that she was or wasn't, why I would; in the meantime, I had framed up with the girl to place it on one of her cousins that she had visited with during the summer. She said her cousin had sexual intercourse with her all right but that he didn't—he said he just barely did get it in. Kinda of a tussle match, you know. The girl was willing to claim that the boy had got her that way, and it was just about her time. I was going to help her through and I told her she could go ahead and lay it to this boy and marry this boy, and if she didn't get along, she could come back home, but her mother was awfully quiet about it and didn't say nothing about me. She said nothing to me more than she got kinda indifferent, and actually I think the girl told her mother; I think the girl spilled on me because she got saulky with me and once there, just awhile before this happened, we had a chance to have sexual intercourse, and she refused me and wouldn't give me no cause for it. I asked her then if she figured on staying with me and keeping our secret or going to turn me down, and she wouldn't give me no answer. That is why I figured on hiking out. If my wife had let me gone, I would have gone and I wouldn't have left a disgrace on the girl.

I make the foregoing statement of my own free will and accord and have signed the same in the presence of witnesses whose named also appear hereon."

(signed) Geo. J. Hassell

One can only wonder if Judge Tatum called a recess after that testimony to let passions subside and prepare for other witnesses. What was going on in that courtroom? Had anybody felt faint or left the courtroom because of the gruesome details? What was going on in the minds of the Fergusons who were listening to this confession in the words of a man they now despised?

Hassell had accused his step-daughter of being promiscuous, not just with him but also with an unidentified cousin. If accurate it could have happened in Colorado, probably during a Ferguson family reunion. There were many male cousins in the family, and this shocking revelation no doubt mortified the deeply religious Susie. And now to hear this dark secret in open court must have been humiliating for Susie's family sitting near the front of the courtroom. I was beginning to understand why my mother had said so little about this murder.

In assessing Hassell's confession, he minimized his actions and failed to explain why he just didn't disappear before Aldon returned home from Clovis.

To me the confession begged for more explanations from this man who annihilated his family. The court pushed on to the next witness.

The Prosecution

Thomas and Susan Hassell and their children, except Sammy.
Photo Provided by Lana Payne Barnett

The Hassells seemed like a very nice family to neighbors. Jurors often hear testimony from witnesses who tell of being completely surprised by the actions of a criminal defendant who does something so seemingly out of character.

Two points were clear in emerging testimony: George Hassell certainly didn't look or act as a murderer; Susan and her children were nice people and didn't deserve to die. These generalizations would come to jurors and spectators still shell-shocked by the news of these killings that occurred only weeks before.

After the confession was read, the next witness called was identified as Mrs. Hamlin, who I later learned was named Kate. It is important to note that Mrs. Hamlin's husband, James, was one of the most important figures in Farwell's history. He had many real estate holdings. And his wife probably knew the Hassell family better than any other.

DIRECT EXAMINATION BY MR. RICHARDS

"My name is Mrs. J. D. Hamlin, and I live near Farwell. I know the defendant, George J. Hassell. He lived on and worked a place of ours during last year. He moved on that place just at Christmas 1925.

"I am also acquainted with the family, each member of the family. There were seven children, I believe. No, there were eight of the children. Aldon was the oldest. He was a boy.

"I had charge and supervision over the place and looked after it. The house is just a small five-room house; and there is a barn and a well on the place. The place is, let me see, I think it is five miles or four, four or five miles due east of Farwell.

"Yes, sir, I know Mr. Hassell pretty well and saw him many times during the last year, many times. I haven't any idea how many.

"Mrs. Hassell was a very good woman and motherly—a splendid woman.

"Mr. Hassell made a crop on the place last year. It was a good crop, and I would say he should have got for that crop something like twelve hundred dollars, but I rather think he got more. That does not include the wheat. He had some wheat, and that wheat crop was worth probably more than thirteen or fourteen hundred dollars for that crop in addition to the wheat, which was worth about $600. That is approximately.

"I knew Maudie Hassell. That was the oldest girl. I saw her frequently, and she was about fifteen or sixteen-years-old. She was a big girl and might have been more than that, but I believe she was about sixteen.

"You ask me if I ever saw Maudie and Mr. Hassell working in the field together. Well I saw them go to the field once I think about the time they finished up with their crop. I remember I was there, and Maudie just finished washing the dishes, and Mr. Hassell called her, and I think they went together.

"Along the latter part of November and December, I missed this family from that place. I missed them on the Friday or Saturday following Thanksgiving. I missed them the following week after Thanksgiving week, to the best of my recollection. That would have been somewhere near the first of December, and that is when I first missed them. So I asked Mr. Hassell where his family was. I asked him where his family was, and he told me they had gone to Shallowater. Let me see, yes, that was the first days in December that he told me they had gone to Shallowater. I saw Mr. Hassell a few days after that, and he told me they had gone to 'Oklahoma.' Well then I saw him another time and asked him the same thing, and he said they went to Oklahoma and he said Mrs. Hassell took her household effects, rented a house in Oklahoma, and put the children in school. He said, 'That is all we can give our children, Mrs. Hamlin, is an education.'"

"You ask me if along about that time I went into this house. No, sir, I did not. It was just a square, I think it was a square, a square hole in the ground about four or five feet deep. It was about ten or twelve feet square. It was a big place, possibly larger than that. The pit was very close to the back door of the house. It was about six or ten feet from the house – very close.

It was on the east side. I noticed it all fall and saw the pit being dug there for several weeks. I never knew or understood what it was being dug for. You ask me if there was any other pit or dug-out there on the premises. Yes, there was a dug-out in which Mrs. Hassell had used for canned fruits and preserves. That was already on the place.

"I think the boys dug this new pit; I saw them digging it—Mr. Hassell's own boys; I think Russell and Virgel. I saw them digging that pit, but I don't remember that I ever saw Aldon or Mr. Hassell either, but I saw the other boys. That was in the fall sometime.

"Yes, sir, Mr. Hassell was a pretty good worker around the place. He was good about keeping up on improvements about the place, and he would come to me occasionally for materials that he wanted in the way of hinges and so forth to fix doors, steps, and so forth, posts, sire, gates, chicken coops—everything. I gave Mr. Hassell those things many times and I would arrange for the material. But he never asked me for any materials to furnish this storm cellar with; he never did mention that pit to me, never."

For those who didn't know about what Mrs. Hamlin was soon to testify, the event would further reveal George Hassell's depravity. Once he cleaned up the blood and gore of his rampage, Hassell was about get rid of any evidence that his family existed in that house. He was going to hire an auctioneer and sell everything, she testified.

"I was present over there on the day of the sale. That was Wednesday, the 22nd of December. There was a good many people there, a big crowd. Mr. Hassell sold everything in the way of implements and household goods and so forth. I saw the sale being made and also saw the hand bills he circulated prior to the sale, advertising the sale. He brought them to me I should say several days before the sale—the last of the week before it or even before that. Maybe Thursday or Friday it was he came to my house and gave me a hand full of the bills and talked over the sale.

"State's Exhibit Number Two, which you had hand (sic) me, is one of the hand bills he used to advertise the sale.

"I think he sold practically all of the stuff mentioned on that hand bill on the day of the sale. I think I see every item here, except as he says 'Other things too numerous to mention.' Miscellaneous stuff.

"I saw him selling canned fruit at that sale that he got out of the cellar. I also saw them sell the quilts; there were about four or possibly six new quilts. Or it could have there were just four of the new quilts, quilts that had not been used. And I saw him sell a little child's bed there.

"The pit we have been talking about, on the day of the sale was packed—filled up and packed evenly, so that a great many of the people at that sale didn't know there was a dug-out there. It was filled in as level as a table. The sale took place I suppose twenty or thirty feet north of that pit, very close.

"I went in the house that day, but didn't see any lady's clothes."

She then added a detail that others would testify about. Something that in retrospect should have aroused suspicion.

"Mr. Hassell came to my house in December sometime and had dinner at our house. That was reasonably early in December, but I do not know exactly when. And at that time, his face and hands were badly scratched up, his face and the backs of his hands. You could plainly see that they were finger-nail scratches. That was early in December. You ask me how he came to eat with us that day. Well he was hauling a lot of corn, and I went to his barn, and he said he was batching (*probably meaning stacking and collating*), which I knew, and so I said 'Come into the house to eat your dinner.' We had already eaten our dinner, but I gave him his dinner; and while he was eating, I saw his face and hands and asked him about it. I said 'What in the world has happened to your face and hands?' I asked him that, and he said he fell off of his pony in the stubble field. And I never asked him any more about it.

"Aldon was a grown boy; I guess he was twenty-one or two. The youngest one—Sammie—was a baby, I think about two-years-old.

"They served a dinner out there the day of the sale. The dinner was spread out to the north of the pit, towards the front of the house.

"Yes, I remember the incident of the bodies being dug up out of the pit on Christmas Eve day. Mr. Lindop had control of the premises then, N. A. Lindop; he had bought Mr. Hassell out and rented the place from me. That was on December 24th that day they dug up the bodies, but Mr. Lindop had rented the place from me before that. On that day, however, he was in possession.

"The place is in the State of Texas and the County of Parmer—where Mr. Hassell lived and made a crop and where these bodies were found.

"I just saw two of the bodies after they were taken out. I saw the two babies; the baby and the child next to him. I saw them as they lifted them out of the dug-out. I didn't see the others then or any time afterwards. No, sir, I didn't see Aldon."

CROSS-EXAMINATION By Mr. Russell

"Yes, sir, I said Mrs. Hassell was a very good woman, and those were splendid children.

"Before this thing happened, Mr. Hassell's conduct toward the family, so far as I observed, was very good. The family seemed to get along perfectly so far as I knew and as far as my observation is concerned. I hadn't observed anything that would indicate any dissention or trouble in the family or anything to arouse suspicion.

"I made inquiry as to the family about the time I missed them, and Mr. Hassell informed me that they had gone to Shallowater, that is in Oklahoma—no, that is in Texas, nine miles this side of Lubbock. Mr. Hassell continued to live on the place after I made inquiry concerning the family, living in the same house batching and using the same premises.

"At the time I inquired of him regarding the whereabouts of his family, he didn't show the slightest indication of nervousness or excitement or distress but appeared to be perfectly normal; neither did he show any signs of nervousness, excitement, or distress when I asked him about his hands and face being scratched. He just told me he had fallen off his pony in the stubble field. He did not at any time show the slightest indication of nervousness but answered me as casually as was possible, and there didn't seem to be any difference in his actions and conduct from what they were prior to that time. There wasn't a thing in the world to arouse any suspicion from his actions.

"No, Mrs. Hassell never mentioned the dug-out to me. No one ever mentioned the dug-out to me. I, however, did make inquiry regarding it one time, the last night I was at Mrs. Hassell's. It must have been Friday or Saturday night before they disappeared. I passed by and called back to her. She stopped at the edge of the dug-out. My car was close to the chicken house, and I was waiting for Mr. Hassell, but he didn't come. And I called back to Mrs. Hassell and asked her how she got that splendid work done, and I commented on it, and that was the only time anybody mentioned that dug-out to me. She did not make any reply to me—oh, yes, she made a reply, but she answered me some way—chatting—I don't know or really remember just what she said."

It is unclear what all the testimony about the dug-out was about, except to speculate that the prosecution may have thought Hassell had been plotting the massacre and planning to bury his family there for some time, although there was no proof.

Nobody seems to know the purpose of the dug-out since Mrs. Hassell already had a cellar for her canned goods and other supplies. Mrs. Hamlin continued her narrative.

"The wheat crop was sold a few days before the sale; I don't remember just how long before. I have reference to the growing crop that he sold and got about $600 for. The other crop I spoke about what (sic) the row crop, which I estimated to be worth twelve or thirteen hundred dollars. He sold all of that crop in town at the elevator, except what he kept for food, and that was sold at the sale. He sold that grain crop pretty early, possibly in October, the last of October. He, of course, received the money for that a considerable period of time before the first of December.

"I don't remember him making any comment about the fruit that was sold at the same being his wife's. Neither did I hear him make any comment about a match safe that was on the wall. I know what you have in mind, but I only 'heard' that."

Reference to the so-called "match safe" is never explained.

"I was there practically all the time the sale was going on. I think I left about 4:30 or five o'clock.

"As I said before, I couldn't tell a bit of difference in Mr. Hassell's conduct after this alleged occurrence, not in the slightest."

One thing is crystal clear about Mrs. Hamlin's testimony: She paid close attention to her tenants and kept an eye on her property, as well as Hassell's farming business. However, she said she was not suspicious, even about Hassell's fingernail scratches.

The prosecution used Mrs. Hamlin's testimony to enter into evidence the list of items Hassell sold at his auction: two horses, thirteen cows, thousands of bundles of feed, two farm wagons, two pitch forks, two scoop shovels, about seventy chickens, three hogs, cooking stove, washing machine, beds, phonograph and records, .22 caliber rifle, and a .12 gauge shotgun, plus "other things too numerous to mention."

After Mrs. Hamlin's testimony was completed, the court took a dinner recess and reconvened at 7:30 P.M. for a rare night court session.

The next witness, J. O. Ford, who lived about a mile east from the Hassell farm, testified that he had known George Hassell and his family for about a year since the Hassells rented the Hamlin farm.

"Yes, sir, I know Mr. Hassell and have known him somewheres in the neighborhood of a year; I don't know exactly. And I was acquainted with all the larger members of the family but didn't really know the children. In particular, however, I was acquainted with Aldon. Aldon told me he was twenty-one-years-old this fall. Aldon would weigh about 165 pounds; that would be my rough estimate of it.

" I knew Mrs. Hassell, too, and I would pass the place there and see them once in a while, going to town. I passed the house and saw them frequently.

"Along during December 1926, along towards the middle of December, I saw something about that place that attracted my attention. I passed on the morning of the 14th of December, a very wet morning after there had been a very drizzling rain and some snow, and there was a fog the next morning; and I saw a big fire there by the hour the next morning and I saw a big fire there by the house. I stopped to see Mr. Hassell. He promised to do some work for me. We were on kind of a trade for him and the boys to do some work for me when he got up with his work, and I stopped for that reason. I saw the fire before I stopped. I got out of the car, he left the fire and come down and met me down about the barn before I got to where he was. I stopped my car right in front of the lane gate that leads up towards the house, right in the opening of the lane where it leads away from the highway, going north, and at that time Mr. Hassell was north and east of the house. The fire also was north and east of his house, I suppose about thirty yards, about the edge of the garden fence, about there. From where I was, I could not see what he was burning, but it was a big fire, about a six-foot blaze.

"I said it was wet and rainy that morning. This was about 8:30, I judge. It had been raining the day before and snowed the night before, kind of a drizzling rain—not much.

"Mr. Hassell had something in his hand, which he was punching in the fire, a stick or an iron, I don't know what it was. And when I stopped my car, he came towards me walking in a pretty good gait—not in a run but a pretty good walk. I reckon I got about thirty yards from the road, about the end of the barn when he met me, and we had our conversation there. He came on to the gate with me—after we met, we turned, and he went back to the gate with me, and we stood there and talked.

"Mr. Hassell coming down there and meeting me that way at that place is what caused me to stop and kept me from getting up to the house. However, that did not create in my mind any serious suspicion. I asked him, when I got to him, what he was doing with such a fire – asked if he was killing a hog, and he said, 'No, just burning trash.' And I said in a joking way, 'Your wife run you out of the house, and you are building a fire to keep warm.'"

Hassell did not seem amused and replied that they were in Oklahoma.

"That was on or about the 14th of December.

"Then we talked about the farm work, and he told me the boys were gone and he didn't think he would be able to do the work for me.

"Well we came on to town that day, and he talked to me about his having a sale; he was contemplating a sale of his stock. The (sic) is the first I knew of his folks being gone or that he had any idea about the sale. He looked like he was bothered some about the sale. I just supposed he was bothered about his folks being gone. And I didn't see anything more of him then for a few days, until the day of the sale. That is about the next I noticed of him, the day of the sale. I attended the sale, and there was a large crowd there. I saw them selling various articles there, among which were some quilts. However, I didn't see the sale of the quilts because I was away from the premises at that time, but I saw them piled up out there."

What was with this business about the unused quilts that were for sale? Hassell had buried some of the victims in bloody bedding where he had beaten them. Quilts were extremely valuable to families at that time and today are considered folk art. I have several quilts my grandmother made, and they have been appraised at thousands of dollars apiece.

"I saw them sell a gun. It was a single-barreled shot gun that carried two shells. He (Mr. Hassell) showed it to the people and explained it; he got two shells in it and showed them how it worked."

This verbal picture is pretty chilling. A mass killer is standing in front of a large crowd close to the home where he had slaughtered his family and is holding the murder weapon for all to see as he describes how it fires.

"It was that day that I saw something that created some suspicion in my mind. I saw something that made me think something was wrong. What I thought about it was that him and his family had some trouble and they had gone for some cause and he was walking out. I thought he was selling out to get away with the money is what I thought."

DEFENSE COUNSEL: "We object to what he thought."

JUDGE: "Sustain that objection. Gentlemen, you will not consider that."

Ford resumed his testimony. "Well I stayed there through the sale that day. That was on the Wednesday before Christmas. I don't know the exact day of the month.

"The next thing that came to my mind that caused suspicion was hearsay, but that wouldn't be admissible.

"But I was at the place again after the 22nd of December. I was there Christmas Eve day, the 24th. The occasion of my being there at that time was to dig out that cellar. The day before this, after I got my suspicions aroused by this hearsay, I came to town and told the officers about what I had heard and seen, and they had started an investigation, and that morning then, the morning that we dug the cellar, that was Christmas Eve morning. Mr. Lendop (sic) came to my house—

"Objection!"

Ford continued: "I came to town and met Mr. Martin (sheriff) out there, and he told me to dig out that cellar that morning, told me to get up a crew of men with shovels, and I did.

"Well I got some men that was on my place, and Mr. Lindop's boys promised to help us. We had some shovels—two, I think, to start with. And Mr. Lindop showed me about where the cellar was, but I had to dig a while before I found where the cellar was. We finally located it, and me and my boy and another one or two went to digging. We dug about two feet down and found some quilts.

"At this time, there were no people there, but a crowd began to gather afterwards.

"We shoveled off a little dirt, about one foot square, about these quilts, and I put a knife out to cut through the quilt to see what was under there, and one man told me not to cut through it but to wait until the officers came. About that time, Mr. Martin came up to the place, and I asked him if he cared for me cutting through there, and he said no, so I did. I cut right through the quilt and on top of something – I didn't know what until I pulled it out. But it exposed a baby's hand and arm to the elbow. I pulled that much up through the slit in the quilt, and it afterwards developed to be a baby – a small baby about two-years-old, I suppose.

"Mr. Martin was standing there then and he said, 'That is enough,' he said, 'Go to Clovis and send an undertaker out,' and we stopped digging. But after a minute, we decided to dig all of the dirt off of the top and have it ready for the undertaker to take the bodies out. So we did, but we didn't remove the quilts.

"The undertaker came afterwards and took the bodies out of the pit. There were nine bodies taken out of that pit.

"I recognized Mrs. Hassell and Aldon and Virgil (sic) and Maudie. Aldon was the oldest boy. His position in the pit was on the east side. His feet were towards the south, and he was laying parallel with the east wall of the cellar, right against the wall. Yes, he was taken out of the pit with the other bodies, and the bodies were placed on some boards beside the house for an hour or so, then put in the ambulance and brought to town. I didn't see the bodies after that time; I didn't see them no more.

"No, I didn't notice particularly the nature of the wounds on Aldon's head, but I noticed that his head was crushed, but I didn't know just where the wounds were that did it or what it was. I remember his forehead being crushed in.

"The undertaker was present when the bodies were taken out. And I think Mr. Martin was present, and Mr. Hawkins, the Deputy, was there.

"No, sir, I didn't see anybody drive up in a wagon or automobile near the edge of that pit on the day of the sale and see Mr. Hassell motion them back. I didn't see that."

According to this last bit of information, there were people at the auction who quickly offered bits of information to authorities after Hassell's arrest. Had any wagon or automobile suddenly got stuck or sank into the pit where the bodies were buried, that would have resulted in a macabre scene. George may have not considered this despite his thorough planning and cleanup of the murder scene.

Defense counsel Russell began cross-examination, but his question is not recorded.

"I think it was December 14th that I said I saw the fire on Mr. Hassell's place. I said he was burning something on a wet foggy morning. He had something in his hand that he was stirring the fire with, and when I stopped, he came to meet me.

"He seemed to be bothered by something, didn't appear quite as jovial as ordinarily.

RUSSELL: "You and he came on to town that day I believe you said."

FORD: "I came to town, and I think I saw him in town that day, yes, sir."

RUSSELL: "When was it you said you and he came to town together, when you was talking about the sale?"

FORD: "I didn't say we came to town together."

RUSSELL: "Oh, I misunderstood you then."

FORD: "I think it must have been, oh, three or four weeks, maybe longer than that before, that he made arrangements with me to do some work for me. In fact I talked to him several times about it. I don't know just the dates. But I wanted some help and so they were getting along pretty well with their work and I asked him for help, and he said he thought they could help me out. I had more than one discussion with him about it, and each time he went right ahead and talked to me about helping me, and I understood that he was going to help me.

"I never visited the family; I have stopped there and talked to Mr. Hassell but never went in the house. But from all that I saw and observed, I never saw anything that would indicate any friction in the family whatever. They seemed to get along pleasantly. I might say one thing, since I thought of it. One time me and my wife passed, and I stopped to see Mr. Hassell about something and I started back to the car—this was along last summer—and this girl, Maudie, came and called me and asked if we were going to Clovis any time that week, and I told her I thought we would, and she said if we did, Mrs. Hassell wanted to go along to Clovis. Perhaps I better not say what I figured."

RUSSELL: "Probably not. But you didn't figure that or anything else looked funny until you heard about this occurrence, did you?"

FORD: "Oh, at that time I didn't think it looked quite right because we wasn't acquainted, just barely knew them. We hadn't been neighbors hardly six months at that time. We weren't their nearest neighbors. I had two neighbors closer than they. It is not a fact that I didn't think about that until after I heard about the occurrence; I thought that was suspicious at the time.

"On the 14th day of December, when I saw the fire there at the place, is when Mr. Hassell told me his family was in Oklahoma, and that is the first I knew about them being away."

RUSSELL: "Now between that time, or a short time prior to the Hassell sale, hadn't you seen and talked to Mr. Hassell at a sale your son had?"

FORD: "We talked about the sale the morning we saw the fire. Mr. Hassell was at my son's sale, which sale took place the day before Mr. Hassell's. I didn't notice anything particularly about him in regard to him being troubled or bothered, didn't notice anything at all.

"As far as I know, Mr. Hassell stayed and remained there on the premises all during the time I have testified about.

"I observed Mr. Hassell's conduct on the day of the sale but didn't notice anything at that time, in regard to his conduct, that aroused my suspicion, only he seemed to be in a hurry. But that didn't create any great amount of suspicion in my mind. I didn't observe anything about him, especially out of the ordinary at any time.

"Yes, sir, I saw Mr. Hassell frequently during the year that I knew him."

RE-DIRECT EXAMINATION BY MR. RICHARDS

"Yes, sir, I passed Mr. Hassell's place nearly every day and therefore had frequent occasion to notice his method of work and his business methods in connection with making improvements around the place and so forth, and I will say that he did his work in a business-like manner I thought. I thought he was about the best renter to fix up a place that I ever saw.

"I noticed something about his work or system of business that seemed to be out of the ordinary or abnormal. It seemed like he was very systematic in his farming and fixing up of the place. He takes a fresno (sort of a grader) and leveled up the holes on the place; and I thought that was out of the ordinary. Not many land owners themselves do that. He was just an all-around good worker, one of the best I ever saw."

RE-CROSS EXAMINATION BY MR. RUSSELL

"Yes, sir, I think it is extraordinary for a renter to take such care of a place. In fact I never saw a renter do so much. I never saw a man fill up holes in the fields before in my life. It is unusual for anybody to do that; I never saw it before.

"I don't know that I ever saw anything else about his methods and actions out of the ordinary. I did not admire his farming, that is, his method. I admired his 'get-up' and 'go.' I liked that. But his method of cultivating his crop, I didn't like that. I didn't think he did that part of it right.

"There was no particular occasion that I know of for him taking his fresno and filling up the holes in the fields that I spoke of, but I went over and wanted to borrow his fresno, and he said he had to use it for that purpose.

"I am a practical farmer and have been farming myself about thirty-four years, and I didn't like Mr. Hassell's method of cultivating. Based on my experience as a farmer, I will say that I think it helps all right to fill up depressions in the fields; I think it is beneficial, but it is out of the ordinary for people to do that.

"He didn't cultivate his crop like I would my own."

RE-DIRECT EXAMINATION BY MR. RICHARDS

FORD: "He just didn't do it like I would have done it."

(WITNESS EXCUSED)

By the time Mr. Ford finished his testimony, the unusual night session must have dragged on until very late. It's hard to figure why there was so much testimony regarding Hassell's farming techniques. Perhaps, the prosecutor was trying to explore if Hassell showed any quirks or evidence of an unstable mind.

The next witness had compelling and chilling testimony.

"My name is N. A. Lindop, and I now live where Mr. Hassell formerly lived, on Judge Hamlin's place east of town. During the last year, I lived just a mile up the road on what is known as the White farm, a mile and a half east of that place.

"I am a man with a family.

"I know Mr. Hassell and knew him during last year and made a crop there by him, farming the land there a mile and a half from him.

"We moved to the Hassell place on Monday before he had the sale on the 22nd. It was on Monday, and you can figure up what date it was.

"Shortly before that, I had made a trade with Mr. Hassell. He had sent me word on Saturday, the 11th, that he wanted to sell me some cows—sell out to me. I didn't just understand it, but I paid very little mind until the next morning, Sunday morning, I got up, and me and the wife was talking, and she said, 'Let's go talk to him about it.' That was the 11th. So we talked with him, and he priced his stuff to me, his wheat and farming tools, and so I told him I would let him know later on.

"I afterwards did buy his wheat, which wheat was a growing crop on the place, and I paid him \$600 for his wheat. How it came about, I went back to see him on Monday and I went to talk with Mrs. Hamlin to see if it would be satisfactory with her because I bought it with a view of taking over the place and making another crop. Well she said it would be all right, so I came back to Mr. Hassell a little while later and told him I would be back Monday morning. He was asking \$600, and I offered him \$500. And I came back Monday morning. It was to be at nine o'clock. But it was cold that morning, and I had a Ford car and couldn't get it started, and I never got over there until about eleven o'clock, and he had gone to town. So I followed him to town, and when I met him, he had backed out on me, and I told him if he wanted to, I would give him \$600 for the wheat and take up the note of \$600 against the implements, and he backed out on me, and I went back home.

"Tuesday I went to town, and he came into Parker's store and said he would trade. So I put up a \$50 forfeit and gave him a check for $50 and came back Wednesday and finished the deal. And I paid him for the wheat and taken up that note, transferred the note.

"After that, on or about the 20th of November (sic; meant December), Monday, I moved my family on the place. I did not see Mr. Hassell's family around there at that time. To be honest with you, I don't know when I had last seen the family, but it had been sometime before that. I couldn't tell you when.

"After we moved in on the 20th, Mr. Hassell continued to stay with us there. I told him he could set his things back to one side, and I would board him free of charge until he had his sale and got away. He had groceries there and everything and furnished his part.

"On Sunday, the 12th, we looked through the house, and the Defendant, Mr. Hassell, was there at that time. He was scrubbing the floor, mopping, or whatever you call it. We could tell he had scrubbed some of the floors, and he said he had scrubbed three rooms. But I never paid any particular attention to that myself. I noticed some of the floors were wet. He had been cleaning them because they were clean and he told he had.

"We didn't get to see all of the rooms at that time. One room he told me was piled up and hadn't been straightened up. That was the middle room on the back side. There was nothing to prevent me from going in that room, except that Mr. Hassell stood in the door. I don't remember what sort of position he was in, but he was standing in the door or just inside; I wouldn't be positive, but he was standing at the door or just inside. He had a mop and a bucket there.

We never did get to see in that room.

"After we moved in, Mr. Hassell continued to sleep there, and he slept in the east room of those three back rooms. You know, the house is three rooms long behind and two rooms in front and a little porch on the south side. Mr. Hassell slept in the east room. He had a bed to sleep on up until he had his sale. It was an iron bedstead. After the sale, he slept on a feather bed made down on the floor.

"During that time, he ate at the table with us when he was there. He missed some meals. He was at town sometimes. But he was generally there and ate with us. I recall that he ate a little supper on the night of the 23rd, before Christmas. I didn't observe him doing anything at all around the house, just sitting at the table figuring something, at the dining table figuring on a little book or something; I never looked at it.

"He never ate a hearty supper that night like had been eating. He didn't go to town that night. He got in the car and put it in the shed and came back to the house. After he had done that, we all went to bed after we had sat around for a little while; I don't know how long. We went to bed somewhere around nine o'clock or later. I don't know the time.

"Yes, sir, I will say that at that time I did have a suspicion in my mind as to his family, which suspicion was created by the way they left here. We didn't see any women's clothing in the house."

What Lindop had testified to was rather spooky. Hassell was stilling living in a farmhouse where he had murdered his family and was planning a big sale of his remaining household goods. His demeanor was beginning to arouse suspicion. Planning a farm auction on property where a mass murder had just occurred takes the height of arrogance and a morbid pathology.

"Well that night of the 23rd, Mr. Hassell made down his bed and went to bed; it was a mattress and a feather bed that belonged to me. He had his own quilts and blankets. He retired sometime between nine and ten o'clock that night. I never looked at the clock, but it was around nine o'clock. Mr. Hassell went to bed about the time we did. I rested pretty well the fore part of the night, but after that, for some reason I woke up. I felt that I had been awake about two hours before I got up, and I got up somewhere between three and four o'clock. I heard something in the other room that aroused me, something in Mr. Hassell's room. Well that didn't wake me though; I was awake when I heard it. I thought he was getting up to make a fire; and my wife told me to get up and make it because he didn't understand the stove. I called him to know what time it was—my clock had stopped—and he told me five o'clock. I got up and made the fire, and the stove was hot and the room was getting warm, and he called me in the room to him, Mr. Hassell did. And I went in, and he told me to get him a doctor, so I went back and told the boys to get a doctor for Mr. Hassell. I couldn't tell you how long I had been back there, but it seemed like a very few minutes when he called me back the second time. The second time, he asked me if the boys was gone, and I told him yes. He said to hurry with the doctor and he said that I wouldn't do anything. He called me back the third time, and the third time he whispered, 'Mr. Lindop, it is this old whiskey; don't excite your wife. Get the doctor and bring Jim Martin.' I asked him who Jim Martin was, and he told me the Sheriff. And when he told me that, I shut the door between us, reached for the baby and the blanket, got the wife and children and everybody in the car, and left that place right now! We got to Judge Hamlin's about 4:30 and aroused them and sent them to town, and I think my boy phoned the doctor and the Sheriff and they went out there.

"I went out to the premises again on the morning of the 24th; I couldn't tell you just what time I got there. To be honest with you, I was there tolerably early, but I couldn't tell you what time. I was there though when they started digging that pit. At the start, there weren't so many people there. They were just beginning to dig the pit when I got there, and I was there all the time they were digging.

"I did not see them take the bodies out of that pit, and I never saw any of the bodies that were taking out. Neither did I see the bodies afterwards, and I never attended the funeral. I had an opportunity to see them and could have seen them if I wanted to"

CROSS-EXAMINATION BY MR. RUSSELL

"I could not tell you when I had seen Mr. Hassell prior to Saturday the eleventh when he wanted to sell me some stuff, but it had been some little bit; I couldn't tell you.

"Me and the wife went over to the place the morning of the 12th, Sunday morning, and looked the premises over, looked through the house, and he told us he had been scrubbing, and the floors looked like he had been scrubbing that morning. That was the morning of the 12th, and the floors looked like he had been scrubbing that very morning.

"And he told me that one room was piled up. The door to that room wasn't open. I suppose we were six or eight feet from the door; he was four or five feet from it. He was standing four or five feet from the door of the room that he said was piled up. He was some considerable distance from the door when he made the remark that the room was piled up. That was the 12th.

"I heard Mr. Ford testify about Mr. Hassell having a big bon fire on the morning of the 14th, but I didn't see none of that."

RUSSELL: "We are going to assume that he was burning the clothes on the 14th; I am going to assume that he was burning those quilts and so forth. And I am also going to assume that those mattresses and quilts were in that room on the 12th when you were there. Now what was there or what did he do other than you stated to keep you from going into that room?"

LINDOP: "Nothing but tell me that."

"And stood four or five feet from the door. I don't know whether he was standing inside or just in it. I couldn't tell positively."

RUSSELL: "Now I understand this calamity occurred on the 6th day of December."

LINDOP: "I don't know."

RUSSELL: "And you say there was fresh evidence of scrubbing on the morning of the 12th."

LINDOP: "Yes, he told me he had scrubbed three rooms and was finishing up.

"I did not see any signs of fresh blood stains on the floor, not a bit. I did not notice a thing unusual or out of the ordinary in his conduct.

"I asked him something about his family, and he said they had gone to Oklahoma. He told me they didn't like it here, that they were dissatisfied.

"I spell my name L-I-N-D-O-P.

"There wasn't anything in this man's conduct that I saw, or in his talk, during the previous negotiations I had with him about the sale of the wheat and the farming tools, from the time I was ever there on the 12th, during the sale or any time, until the morning of the 24th. There was nothing to impress my mind that he had killed nine people. I don't think that I ever knew or saw any man prior to that time that had killed anybody, so I have not had any experience in that line.

"I bought this wheat from him on the Wednesday before the day of the sale the coming Wednesday, one week before. Well I bought it on Tuesday, but we closed the deal, and I paid him on Wednesday. I gave him $600 cash for the wheat and gave him a check on a local bank, namely The Guaranty State Bank of Farwell. He had $600 against his farming tools that he owed Emerson-Birmingham Company, and he transferred the note against me, and I assumed the indebtedness. I did not pay him any cash for the farming tools, just took over the debt against them and made that obligation mine and gave him $600 in cash.

"I had learned, of course, that he had sold his grain crop a month or two before that my boys helped haul it off. That was sometime in October, I think, but I don't know for sure. I don't know where he sold it. My boys helped haul it, but I don't know where they sold it. I do not have any idea about the value of that crop. It was sold somewhere along the latter part of October or the first of November, but I couldn't tell you just exactly what time. I don't know what he did with it, but he did dispose of it. And I bought his wheat crop (growing wheat crop) and gave him $600 for it a week before his sale, and he had his sale the following Wednesday.

"Yes, sir, I attended the sale.

"All during the time after we moved into the house on the 20th, I did not notice a thing unusual about Mr. Hassel's conduct. We asked about his family, and he talked naturally about them and went right on as if nothing had ever happened, so far as I could tell. He slept right there in the same house and stayed on the premises all the time after this occurrence, except when he would go to town. And he slept and batched there, so far as I knew, until we moved in. And after we moved in on the 20th, he went ahead in the same manner and act natural, talked to us about his family like if he had nothing on his mind.

"On the morning of the 24th, the third time he called me into his room, he made the remark, 'It is that old whiskey.' I couldn't tell you whether he had been drinking heavily, but he didn't seem to be drunk. I could probably have smelled it on is breath and tell if he had had a drink. As far as his appearance was concerned, I couldn't tell that he was drinking at all, apparently normal.

"There was not a thing in the world on the night of the 23rd to attract my attention when he went to bed. All he did was sit at the table and do some figuring, and I suppose he had done that prior to that time. I never paid any attention to his figuring. I knew he had had the sale, you know, on Wednesday, the day before, and just assumed he was figuring up his sales accounts and paid no attention to him. He went to bed in the usual manner.

"Now in regard to my waking up, it is just as I said a while ago; I had been awake a couple of hours but don't know exactly how long. Nothing woke me that I know of, but I was just awake. I don't know what waked me. I do that sometimes. It must have been somewhere about one o'clock when I woke up. No, I do not have a habit of waking up that way and lying awake at night; when I wake up, I generally grunt and go to sleep again. I do not know why woke up on that particular morning, but I did, and it was unusual for me to lay awake that way for so long. I didn't unconsciously hear any noise to wake me that I know of, but after I had been awake about two hours, I did hear a noise in Mr. Hassell's room. I called him and asked what time it was, and it was five o'clock.

"I got up and made a fire, and the stove was hot and room beginning to get warm, and he called me to his room. It must have been something like twenty or thirty minutes from the time I asked him what time it was until he called me to his room. And he asked me to get a doctor for him. To be honest with you, I don't know whether or not I asked him what was the matter. I asked if I couldn't do something for him, but so far as I remember, I didn't ask him what the trouble was. About that time, I had a suspicion that there was something wrong about his family. That suspicion got into my mind sometime between the 12th and the 19th of December before we moved into Mr. Hassell's place because I knew his family and knew that they were satisfied, so his wife told me and then got up and left you might say in a short while, and I never knew how they left or went—

and I got to studying about it. That idea occurred to me that week, and I discussed it with my wife. No, sir, I didn't discuss it with Mr. Hassell when I went over there the 20th. I gave the matter serious thought all along from then on. That thought struck me the week beginning the 12th.

"I also communicated my suspicions to Judge Hamlin sometime that week. I knew something was wrong. In other words, I didn't believe the family voluntarily moved away as Mr. Hassell had said, and I discussed the matter with Mrs. Lindop, and she agreed with me. And with all of that in my mind, I yet didn't notice anything out of the ordinary about Mr. Hassell, and I was looking at him and watching him with that in mind and still he didn't show any indication of anything being wrong. He talked in a manner that would allay my suspicions, and he about had me convinced that there wasn't anything wrong.

RE-DIRECT EXAMINATON BY MR. RICHARDS

"I lived there all during last year and saw Mr. Hassell's work. I never saw him in the field, but I knew they were working. I wasn't with him so very often; just once in a while I would see him. I didn't see anything out of the ordinary about him all during that year.

"That house has recently been re-papered inside. It was after Christmas that it was re-papered—the next day. It was papered and painted on the inside.

"Yes, sir, I have observed some bloody fingerprints on the door in the house on one place. They are on the door that opens into the little room on the north.

"I knew Mrs. Hassell tolerably well. She was not a grouchy or quarrelsome woman, but she seemed like an awfully fine woman. She was a pleasant woman—just as pleasant when she was around my home and place as she could be."

RE-CROSS EXAMINATION BY MR. RUSSELL

"I didn't know the names of the children, but I had seen them, and they were all pleasant. Mr. Hassell also was a pleasant fellow and a good neighbor. I never noticed anything at all out of the ordinary with the family at any time. They seemed to get along, as well as any average family gets along. I never even heard anybody saw that there was any particular discord in the family, and I never had any such suspicion myself."

Lindop was excused from the witness stand, setting the stage for more testimony about Hassell's call to the doctor and what transpired afterwards. Lindop's seventeen-year-old son, Lester, testified briefly about going to Judge Hamlin's place and summoning the doctor and sheriff. He was asked about the giant pit that had been dug in the yard, adding that he had seen it in October but never heard the purpose for digging it.

Hassell's Story Doesn't Add Up

George Hassell's story about his family's sudden disappearance was arousing more suspicion and consternation among his neighbors.

The county attorney, J. D. Thomas, was recalled to the witness stand and was questioned by prosecutor, Mr. Richards. It was unusual at best in rural Texas, where nothing serious ever seemed to happen, for an important county official to get involved in a criminal investigation. Mr. Thomas proved to be an invaluable witness because he seemed to push the missing family aspect of the case to the fore.

"My name is J. D. Thomas. I believe I stated before that I am County Attorney of Parmer County, Texas.

"I know the defendant, George J. Hassell. I had occasion to have a conversation with Mr. Hassell in my office along about the 23rd of December. I believe Mr. Ford came to my office that morning and told practically the same story that he told on the witness stand with reference to Mr. Hassell and his family and then made known the fact that other parties were suspicious about his family, and we thought we ought to make an investigation.

"I agreed with him, of course, after he told me his story, and I assured him we would make some investigation. Then I believe I talked to the Sheriff next about it, and we went out to see Mrs. Hamlin, and she related about the same story that she told here on the witness stand. And by making other investigation, we found out that Mr. Hassell was coming into town to see Mr. Overstreet I believe to make a settlement with reference to this sale. I told the sheriff to get him, if he could, at that time and bring him over and we would interrogate him. I cautioned him that if he was that bad of a man, he better get another man to go with him, and I believe he did."

Hassell had evaded suspicion for a decade about his other family in Whittier, California. Did he feel a noose tightening around his neck at this point? Psychopaths have no conscience and often think they are smarter than everyone else. He had lied and manipulated people up to this point. Could he do it again?

Thomas continued, "And he (Hassell) came over to Mr. Overstreet's office, and I had arrangements with them to 'phone the office when he came in. Well they 'phoned us, and the Sheriff went after him and brought him up to the office. Mr. Martin and Mr. Hawkins, I believe, came with him. Mr. Hassell was not under arrest at that time; I just interrogated him. No warrant was issued for him, and none of us were exercising any sort of restraint over him at that time, none whatever. We just had him there for a talk, and he didn't know what he was coming there for.

"Well he came in, and I think I asked him a few general questions, where he came from to this country, and he told me he came from Oklahoma. I had never met him before, or at any rate, didn't remember having met him before. I asked him how long he had been in this country and a few things like that, and he told me. Then I told him that he was under suspicion as to the whereabouts of his family. Well he looked rather excited, but I expected that, of course, coming to the County Attorney's office, he would probably (not) be enthused whether he was guilty or not. And he said that he was sure that suspicion was aroused because Mrs. Hamlin interrogating him and that he considered his business his business and her business her business and that he had given her pert answers to her questions and just because he thought she was trying to inquire into his personal affairs. I told him that might be true but that he had given conflicting answers with reference to the whereabouts of his family. I heard he said that they had gone to Shallowater, Texas and also to Blair, Oklahoma. So he told a very plausible tale. He stated that her (Susan) brother, J. D. Ferguson, lived at Perryton, Texas and had come down in a truck, a Chevrolet truck, that they were expecting the Fergusons to come down, but they came at a rather unexpected time, and the family was going to visit another sister's family at Shallowater. They arrived at night and left the next morning. I don't remember just when he said they left, but he undertook to fix that time. And from Shallowater, he said they were going to Blair, Oklahoma.

"And I interrogated him about the cellar, and he said that he dug the cellar because he thought he needed it and later found he didn't need it and that he wanted to leave the premises in as good condition as possible and filled it in.

"I asked him then if he could give me a reference where I might wire and verify his statement, and he stated if I would wire to Jack Scroggins, Blair, Oklahoma, Scroggins would verify his statement that his family was at Blair, Oklahoma. I told him I would do that and asked him to help me clear up the situation because he was under suspicion, and as far as I was concerned, he could go and be at liberty."

The identity of Jack Scroggins is never explained in the county attorney's testimony. However, Hassell had lived briefly in his dead brother's home in Blair, Oklahoma prior to marrying the widowed Susan, and they had lived there briefly as a family before moving to Farwell. Hassell was cagey enough to avoid giving the attorney any name among Susan's vast family of six brothers and four sisters. Scroggins is not listed as any distant relative that I could find. But he could have been an acquaintance that Hassell had hoped would either cover for him or be impossible to track down.

Thomas continued, "Well he (Hassell) left my office, and I immediately wired to the address he gave me. When he got over to Hamlin's office, he phoned and asked me if he might go to the bank. I told him to go anywhere he wanted to. So he went down to the bank. I don't know, but I suppose he did. He said he was. And I wired that afternoon to Jack Scroggins but didn't get any answer that afternoon. I got an answer the next day from Jack Scroggins that the family was not at Blair and that he didn't know anything about them. I afterwards saw Mr. Hassell and told him the purport of the telegram."

RICHARDS: "When and where was that?"

THOMAS: "Well after we had exhumed the bodies and placed them down in the warehouse—in the meantime, Mr. Hassell had gone to Clovis in very weakened condition so that the doctors had to operate on him. He was out in the jail at that time. I believe that was the next day, Christmas day. The day we buried them."

As a distant relative, I am perplexed at this point about why the authorities were in such a hurry to bury the family and had seemingly made no effort to further contact Aunt Susan's family to make notification of the deaths. Even if Farwell or Parmer County had no official morgue, the freezing, wintry conditions would not have affected the decomposition of the bodies.

Thomas continued, "The Sheriff stated to me that Hassell might make a statement. None of us had communicated to him that we had found the bodies. So I went out to the jail and I said to him that I had a return from this wire, that I heard from Jack Scroggins. He said 'You have?' and I said 'Yes, sir.' He said 'What did he say?' I said, 'Well he said that your family wasn't in Blair, Oklahoma and hadn't been there.' Well he said, 'That is strange.' He had previously told me that he had a letter from his wife, so I undertook to let him fix again when he had received that letter. I asked him about this letter, and he said he got that last Monday, I believe it was—still trying to convince me, it seems, that his family had gone. Of course he was in a very weakened condition laying there on the bed. But I looked at him and I told him, 'Mr. Hassell, your family has been found—was found out in the cellar where you placed them after you knocked them in the head with an axe.' So he lay there two or three minutes without saying anything. The first thing he said was, 'Get a doctor and examine that girl.'

"He was very nervous at that time. The sweat was rolling off of him, off of his forehead. I never saw a man in such condition as he seemed to be at that time.

"Then he stated, 'Get a doctor' before trying to explain his acts or anything, he said, 'Get a doctor and have that girl examined.' Then he said the girl was in a family way and made some further remarks about it.

"On the morning of the 24th, when the Sheriff and doctor went out there, I also went with them. When we got out to the place, there was nobody there. We got out there, it seemed like about four or five o'clock. There was snow on the ground, and it was cold, and there were no lights in the house. Mr. Hawkins and Mr. Martin and Doctor Clark, I believe, were in the company. And we had some difficulty getting up to the house, but we finally got up there and hollered at the door, and nobody seemed to be aroused. We went in, and he was lying on his bed and he turned the cover back and said, 'Look what they did to me.' Of course it was easy to see he was lying there in his own blood; he was just as bloody as he could be. The next thing he said, he handed us a knife and said, 'Here is what they did it with.'

"Well the next statement he made I believe was, 'Let's go to a sanitarium and get there quick.' He seemed to give us instructions what to do, and we dressed him and had some difficulty getting his clothes on him. He seemed to be in a very weakened condition and suffering from pain. It was plain to be seen that his wrist was cut and he had some body wounds, which we couldn't at that time ascertain, but his clothes were very bloody.

"Well we put on his clothes, got in the automobile, and took him to Clovis. Mr. Martin and I both went to Clovis with him, and we both came back. We stayed there during the operation that Doctor Smith performed.

"When Mr. Martin and I got back, we went back to the Hassell place. Of course I was fully convinced in my own mind that there had been some foul play and that if we went into that cellar, we would find the bodies. The Sheriff and I discussed it, and we immediately reached the conclusion that the cellar ought to be gone into, and I believe it was stated by Mr. Ford that we saw him in town and told him to get a complete crew and go into the cellar as quickly as possible. I was there all the time they were digging the cellar, and there was a good many other people out there.

"I saw the bodies taken out; there were nine of them. I didn't know any of them and therefore didn't recognize them. I don't remember ever having seen them.

"You ask me to tell the jury about the position the different bodies were laying in the pit. Well the mother and the little children, as I remember it, and the daughter and one of the boys – of course the boy looked like a boy about seventeen or eighteen years of age – were lying on the east side of the cellar covered up with quilts. The baby, I believe – the little baby and some of the other smaller children were on the north side of the cave – not lying close to the others – but it seems like the mother and the daughter and the one that must have been the eighteen-year-old boy was on the west side of the pit. Then on the east side there was a body, that of a boy, I would judge to be nineteen, eighteen, or twenty-years-old, all to himself. And with that body, there was some bedding. I remember seeing the mattress and also the pillow. The pillow was bloody as it would be.

"The body on the east side was buried at a lesser depth than the others, shallower than the others. All of the others were buried at about the same level. But this one of the east side was higher up, and it had some bedding around it, a mattress and a pillow.

"Yes, sir, I saw the boy on the east side after his body was dug up, and I noticed that his skull seemed to have been crushed. Of course I couldn't tell what caused it, but there was a big hole in his forehead.

"I never saw the bodies again after that; I only saw them out on the premises and made whatever examination I wanted to make there. Yes, I attended the funerals but didn't view the bodies.

"I have been out to the Hassell place since that time and found the finger prints on the door. The finger prints were of blood.

"The place where the bodies were taken out is located in the County of Parmer and the State of Texas."

CROSS EXAMINATION BY MR. RUSSELL

"I supposed it was on the 24th of December that Mr. Ford came to my office and communicated his suspicions to us. I don't know for sure whether Mr. Ford came to me first or to Mr. Martin first, but at any rate I told the Sheriff to get the defendant, Hassell, and bring him to my office. When Hassell arrived at my office, I told him he was under suspicion of some foul play as to the whereabouts of his family, and he made some remarks then about Mrs. Hamlin having questioned him about it prior to that. I understood that Mrs. Hamlin had spoken to him in a way that would indicate that she had some suspicion about it, however, Mrs. Hamlin had not at that time conveyed her suspicions to me.

"I don't know that Ford told me that Mrs. Hamlin had suspicioned him, but he said Mrs. Hamlin would give us more facts about the situation—that she knew more about it than anybody else. I had some little discussion with him in my office about it the day after the sale. The sale was on the 22nd, and this discussion in my office occurred on the 23rd of December, about two or three o'clock in the afternoon. Hassell then left my place of business and went down town somewhere and afterwards phoned me and said he wanted to go to the bank, and I told him to go ahead, that he was at liberty to go anywhere he wanted to. As far as I know, he went to the bank then. It must have been about five or ten minutes after he left my office that he called up saying he wanted to go to the bank, and I told him to go ahead as far as I was concerned.

"I didn't make any further investigation on that day. He told me at that time that his family was in Blair, Oklahoma and told me to wire there for the information.

"I did not know at that time that he had a Ford automobile, and of course, I don't know whether the Sheriff knew it at that time. I learned since, however, that he had one. And I since learned that he had sold his crop along in October and sold his growing crop along about the time of his sale and that he got cash for it and that he had had a sale and some little bills to be settled up and that he was probably going to the bank for that purpose when he phoned me. And I learned later that he had some unfinished business with Mr. Overstreet that he hadn't wound up. I since learned, however, that practically all of his business was wound up on the 23rd. And he was in the bank on the evening of the 23rd. So far as I have ever learned, there was nothing to prevent him from drawing his several hundred dollars out of the bank that evening,

"In our conversation that day, I told Mr. Hassell that there were some strong suspicions about him and that they would have to be cleared up."

RUSSELL: "Would have to be cleared up. Well ordinarily if a man knew he was guilty of having taken the lives of nine people and somebody would make that kind of remark to him, the chances are that he would understand what he was talking about, wouldn't he?"

THOMAS: "Likely."

RUSSELL: "Then on top of that, this defendant went back to that place where those bodies were and spent the night of the 23rd and 24th. You learned that. And you found him out there wounded on the morning of the 24th after he had sent word in here to bring the doctor and the Sheriff."

THOMAS: "Yes."

RUSSELL: "And handed you a knife. Didn't you ask him and say, 'Who did what?'

THOMAS: "No, but I did on my way to Clovis."

RUSSELL: "I am speaking of right there when he says 'Look what they did' and so forth. Didn't you or the Sheriff say 'who did?'"

THOMAS: "I believe I asked him that question."

RUSSELL: "What did he say?"

THOMAS: "Well he said 'They.' I said 'Who is they?' and he—it seems to me like he said 'Lindop' or something—I won't be positive about that statement, but he did make some statement with reference to that. He said 'They are in there,' and I said, 'Who are in there?' and he said 'Lindop.' He gave a very unintelligible answer."

RUSSELL: "Oh, I see; he was out of his mind apparently."

THOMAS: "No, but he seemed to be in agony and pain."

RUSSELL: "He gave you an unintelligible answer."

THOMAS: "Yes."

RUSSELL: "Made no sense."

THOMAS: "Not much sense to it. Then we took him to Clovis and had his wounds dressed. I think he stayed in Clovis possibly a day and a night, about a day and a night. He didn't make a confession that day.

"I was right there and saw the operation performed and his wounds dressed. He had lost much blood from his wrist and other wounds, and it was after that that he made the statement 'Get a doctor and examine the girl.' Then he made another statement that I haven't made here."

RUSSELL: "Go ahead and make it."

THOMAS: "He said 'Get a doctor and have the girl examined.' Then he followed that with the statement that one of the brothers—boys—had had intercourse with the girl. Followed with the statement that the boy had intercourse with the mother and that is how the row started. Then I asked him if she had made any accusations against him of having intercourse with the girl, and he said no.

"I don't know whether at that time he knew whether or not he was going to get well. The doctors never told us that his wounds were very serious. When we found Hassell, he had on his night clothes, and we picked him up and carried him to the automobile and put him in it. He fell between the seats and rode in that condition to Clovis. The doctor assured us from the beginning that there was a chance of his recovery. He said the intestines were not punctured—just a stab (sic)—and he said if there wasn't any infection, he would probably get all right. Yes, I know there was the best chance in the world to get infection by handling a man like we did him. We put the dirty clothes back on those wounds; and the chances are the knife blade was dirty. It was in that condition that the defendant said, 'Get a doctor and have the girl examined' and that the other things I have mentioned happened. And it was in that condition that he said on the 24th, in that nervous condition with the sweat pouring off of his forehead.

"So far as I know, Mr. Hassell never made any effort or attempt to escape after what I told him in my office on December 23rd. And so far as I know, he had every opportunity to climb in that Ford car, draw all of his money out of the bank, and go as far as that old car would take him."

So far the trial seems to have moved at break-neck speed with key witnesses, as well as the reading of Hassell's damning confession. Defense attorney Russell attempted to push an angle that Hassell was mentally unstable. Thomas, however, countered that he was merely "nervous" as any guilty man would be after murdering nine members of his family.

The trial was moving far into the night, but the prosecution wanted to finish the first day with Sheriff Jim Martin's testimony.

"My name is J. H. Martin, and I hold the official position of Sheriff of Parmer County, Texas. I held that position during December 1926.

"Yes, sir, I recall having had a call early on the morning of the 24th of December to go to the Hassell place. One of the Lindop boys called me somewhere about four o'clock in the morning. I got up, and Mr. Thomas and Mr. Hawkins went with me directly to the Hassell place. When he got there, we went in. There was no lights. Well we found him in a little back room on the bed all in blood. We lit a flash light so we could see. And he said something like, 'Here is what they done to me and this is what they done it with,' or something to that effect. "I have the knife that he handed to me. Here it is. It is in practically the same condition now as it was at the time, and I have kept it in my custody since that time."

RICHARDS: "We offer the knife in evidence that Mr. Hassell is supposed to have been wounded with, and I wish to exhibit it to the jury."

(Thereupon the knife was marked by the reporter for identification as Plaintiff's Exhibit Number Three). Perhaps the record should have noted that the court clerk made that identification.

MARTIN: "Mr. Hawkins, Doctor Clark, and myself go there about the same time, but we didn't all go in the same conveyance.

"Mr. Hassell handed me that knife and made that remark. Then he asked to be taken to a sanitarium to get relief. I tried to get him to let Doctor Clark dress the wounds there but said he wouldn't, that the room was too cold. So we proceeded to take him to the sanitarium at Clovis, and we left him under the care of Doctor Smith at the Baptist Sanitarium, where he remained until after the operation. We stayed also until they were practically through with the operating. They hadn't taken him out of the operating room, but they were practically through. We left him in the sanitarium and came back.

"I then went right back to Farwell and met Mr. Ford and several others on the street and asked them to make arrangements to dig the cellar out. Then I ate breakfast and went on out myself. I don't think they were digging when I got there; I think I got there about the time they were digging it, and I saw them exhume the bodies and take them out. There were nine of them, all dead. I didn't know the family at all and therefore didn't recognize any of them.

"You ask me to tell the jury as near as I can the position in which the different bodies were lying in the pit. Well I couldn't tell the different ones. Some of them were lying on their faces. Eight of them were on the west side, along the west side of the dugout; some lying on their faces and some on their backs. They were all piled up, laid in there in kind of a systematic order, side by side, with quilts or bedclothing spread over them. Then there was one in the southeast corner that looked to be a grown man in size. I don't believe he was on the same level with the others; at any rate, he wasn't covered quite so deep, but it looked like he was lying on the bottom of the dug-out – out there it hadn't been dug quite as deep.

"Yes, I examined the wounds on the boy's head. I just noticed as he was taken out and looked after he was laid out. The wound was in his head, in the side of his head, and his forehead seemed to be smashed in. The skin wasn't broken as I remember. The skin wasn't broken on the front part, but his head was kind of mashed out this way.

"I said there was a hole in the side of his head, but I don't want to be positive which side; I believe, however, it was this side (indicating left). I will say that it appeared to be the result of a gunshot wound. I was there when they took his body out.

"While they were digging there, they dug an axe out. I saw it taken out. It was located towards the northeast corner of the pit; it was kind of out toward the middle of the dugout. I have that axe."

(Objection sustained to introduction of axe)

"I saw the axe taken out of the pit. It had been buried along with the rest of the bodies.

"After the bodies were dug out, they were taken to town and kept in the warehouse that night and buried Christmas day, all of them, and I did not attend the funeral. Neither was I present the day of the sale.

"The Hassell home is located in the County of Parmer and the State of Texas."

CROSS EXAMINATION BY MR. RUSSELL.

"I said that wound appeared to be gun shot.

"I heard Mr. Thomas' testimony, and I recall that occasion of bringing Mr. Hassell into Mr. Thomas' office on the 23rd of December and recall Mr. Thomas questioning him and telling him that there was some suspicion about where his family was, and I questioned him at some length. He was then permitted to leave and go downtown, and he did leave and go to town.

"No, sir, I did not get in touch with the banker and tell him if Hassell tried to draw out his money to let me know. We turned the man loose after having that talk with him. However, I went to the bank after he had been down there, to see if he did draw any out. But Mr. Hassell was permitted to go his way after that conversation that afternoon.

"I knew at that time that he had a Ford.

"Mr. Hassell went on home about five o'clock, and that was when I last seen him on that day. I didn't see him anymore or pay any further attention until I was called to his home on the morning of the 24th, when he handed me the knife and said, 'Look what they have done to me,' and 'This is what they did it with.' I didn't ask him 'Who did it,' and I don't recall Mr. Thomas asking that. Of course I wasn't present all the time; I went out to the car. But I did hear him make the remark about 'Look what they have done to me' and 'This is what they did it with,' but I didn't ask him any questions about what caused it. I tried to get him to let the doctor dress his wounds; I wanted to take care of him some way. His speech didn't seem to be incoherent at that time.

"I didn't ask him who did what because I didn't want to take up the time. I thought he did it himself anyway because the evening before, I followed him everywhere, he went in town and from everything he said and did, I was fully convinced that he wasn't guilty when he left town. But at that time, after that happened, why, I was convinced that he was guilty. That was the final stroke that convinced me. I never heard of the case until the evening of the 22nd when we had that conversation in Mr. Thomas' office. After he left Mr. Thomas' office, I followed him over to Hamlin Overstreet's and talked to Mr. Overstreet and asked him how he appeared and then I followed him to the bank and saw what he did there and then followed him down to Mr.

Hawkin's office, and from there, he went home. That was about five o'clock in the evening.

"I said, from the time I met him on the afternoon of the 23rd and accompanied him to Mr. Thomas' office, I watched him the balance of the afternoon until he left and went home; and all of his actions, talk, and conduct appeared to be absolutely normal, and there was nothing about it to arouse my suspicion. When he left for home, all of my suspicions were practically allayed. But the next morning, when I went out there and found him wounded, then my suspicions became almost certainties. And that is the reason I didn't ask him who did it. That is the reason exactly.

"Then we took Mr. Hassell to Clovis and brought him back the same evening. We took him over there on the morning of the 24th and brought him back that evening. We then kept him here four or five days; I don't remember exactly.

"Yes, I was present and remember the time Mr. Thomas had his first conversation with him, when he said something about having the girl examined. That was on Christmas day, the next morning. He was in a nervous condition at that time and was suffering apparently and in a weakened condition on account of the loss of blood and from undergoing this operation. After about three or four days, however, he began to gain strength.

"I didn't say he was nervous on the morning of the 25th. He was just up from under the influence of this medicine, and after the operation, I know he was weak. I had an operation myself the week before, and I know how I felt. He didn't feel like talking at all when the County Attorney was out there talking to him.

"Based on my experience with my own operation, I will say that Mr. Hassell appeared like a man who had just gone through an operation, but he didn't seem to be laboring under any mental strain or stress.

"I have been with him pretty much since then, and I have never heard him say that he was mentally disturbed. He always seemed to be in pretty good spirits and laughed and talked with me and the other officers and with the doctor. And he doesn't act like a man that even had any trouble or worry in his life."

RE-DIRECT EXAMINATION BY MR. RICHARDS

"I was present when Mr. Thomas told him about his family being found. He might have appeared under some mental stress that morning. I asked him a question, and he didn't answer for a little bit, but I felt that was due to his condition. After an operation, a man sometimes doesn't want to talk. I don't know whether that was the cause or not; it might have been mental stress."

RE-CROSS EXAMINATION BY MR. RUSSELL

"After a day or two, as soon as he regained some strength, when I would ask him questions, he would answer freely. That particular morning, he made the statement that he felt bad and that he would make a statement when he felt better; and from there on out, he didn't do anything but talk and tell the history of his life and everybody else's, at least part of it, he told us considerable of his history. Every time he gets an audience, he talks and seems to enjoy it; and his words and attitude in all his conversations—he would tell about these various things he has been into with as little concern as you and I would talk about going duck hunting. So far as I am concerned, I have never observed any particular stress, mental stress, or anything that would indicate that the man had ever done a thing in the world wrong."

RE-DIRECT EXAMINATION BY MR. RICHARDS

"I only met Mr. Hassell one time before this occurrence and never had any conversation or dealings with him."

(Witness excused)

The trial was set to begin the next day, Tuesday, January 11th, at 9:55 A.M.

As the all-male jury filed out of the courtroom, their last image of the defendant was of somebody who didn't seem too remorseful after the killings. He was jovial and entertaining his jailors with stories about his life. He seemed rather carefree for a man in his position.

Testimony: Day Two

It had been a dramatic first day of testimony, one that had to be fairly exhausting for everybody involved. A jury had been picked, and hours of testimony had dragged far into the night. Now the second day of trial was underway. Imagine that the community of Farwell, the entire Panhandle, nearby Clovis, and all the surrounding communities in New Mexico were enthralled with what had been documented in court. I can imagine some court spectators hurrying out in the hall and outside to provide the latest bits of testimony to the crowd of concerned citizens.

It is assumed the first witness arrived on time, and testimony began as scheduled. Following Sheriff Martin's testimony, his Deputy R. A. Hawkins was next to the stand to provide more insight into George Hassell. He knew him better than most of Farwell because Hawkins was a businessman, as well as a lawman.

"My name is R. A. Hawkins and hold the official position as Deputy Sheriff and Constable of Parmer County, Texas. I am engaged in the grain business.

"I know George J. Hassell, the defendant; I had occasion to go to the Hassell place on the morning of December 24th. Mr. Martin came to my place and called me and then Mr. Martin and I went and got Mr. Thomas, and we all went to the Hassell place. When we got there, we found Mr. Hassell on the bed in the northeast corner of the house in pretty bad shape. I just don't remember the exact words he used, but it seems like Mr. Hassell said, 'Look what they did to me,' He threw his hands open and said, 'That is what they did it with.' He had the knife in his hand.

"Then he jumped up and said he wanted to go to the sanitarium quick. Some of us suggested that he let the doctor treat his wounds there, and he said, 'No, I wanted to get to the sanitarium quick.' And Mr. Martin moved the car around to the front, and Mr. Thomas and I braced Mr. Hassell, and he walked out to the car and got in the car.

"Doctor Clark also was with us there in the room, but Hassell wouldn't allow him to treat him there, so we took him to the Baptist Sanitarium at Clovis. I believe Doctor Smith was in charge of the hospital. I was present when they started on the operation, and they were pretty well along with it when we left. Then we got in the car and came back to Farwell.

"It was pretty well in the morning by the time we got back to Farwell, and we hadn't had any breakfast, so we went to different places to eat breakfast and then went back to the Hassell place and began digging the pit. We dug up nine bodies. I didn't recognize any of them, except Aldon, one of the boys whom I became better acquainted with than any of the other family. I had seen them all but wasn't personally acquainted with them. Aldon was lying on the east side of the pit, with his feet in the southeast corner. I judge his body was a little bit higher than the rest of them. There was some on the other side, but Aldon was a little higher in the pit than the others, not more than eight inches from the surface, eight or ten inches.

"I saw Aldon taken out of the pit, and I notice a wound on his head; I could see a hole in the side of his head. His head seemed to be flattened and out of shape, but the skin wasn't broken anywhere, except where there seemed to a gunshot wound.

"Yes, sir, I saw the bodies again after that; I looked after them until the undertaker came the next day. I did not attend the funeral myself, but the bodies were buried in Farwell. The undertaker's name was Steed, from Clovis.

"I know Mr. Hassell fairly well. I got acquainted with him just after he came to this country. The Hamlin folks sold him a bunch of feed one time that he weighed over my scales. I am in the feed and grain business myself and do business with the farmers generally. I never had any dealings with him during last fall, however, I did buy the seed that he had left over to make a crop this year, and possibly some corn. I saw him along through the summer and fall frequently and spoke to him. He was in my office quite often. How come me to get so well-acquainted with him: he lost a poney (sic) and came to my office numerous times to inquire about it, and he finally found him.

"I never saw anything in his talk or conduct or actions along during the fall when I was with him, that was abnormal or out of the ordinary. He appeared to be like any other normal man, seemed to be all right and seemed to be all right the last time I saw him before this occurred. I never saw anything out of the ordinary about his conduct.

"He was in my office on the 23rd of December. I had bought quite a bunch of feed, and the trucks were hauling off that stuff that day. Well after we had been to the courthouse, he came back to my office and asked me two or three times about getting the rest of that stuff in, that feed, and we talked around there some little time.

"You ask me if he had any marks or scratches on his face or hands about that time. One time, two or three weeks prior to this time, he did. He was in my office one day, and in a joking way, I said 'How did the other fellow look?' And he said 'Why do you want to know,' or something to that affect, and I said, 'That is the only way that an officer makes any money.' Finally he told me that a horse threw him in a stubble field. The nature of his wounds, as I remember, were scratches. I think one of his hands was tied up a little bit and his face was scratched. He told me that the horse fell in the stubble field.

"I never talked to him since then until after we had him in jail. I don't remember just when that was. Possibly about the day or morning that he made his confession. I don't remember. It might have been earlier. It was along about that time; sometime during the time I was with him in the jail.

"I, personally, never had anything to do with keeping in touch with Mr. Hassell's bank account."

This reference may have related to previous testimony about Hassell's banking after the auction at his home and the sale of his feed inventory. Although it is not part of the record, the prosecution apparently was intrigued with how much Hassell made at the sale and how much he had profited from disposing of his farming operation.

And then the prosecution asked another question that moved in a completely new direction.

"The ring you hand me, I have seen before. That was on Mr. Hassell's finger. When we got him from out there, it was on his finger until while he was here in jail, and he said something about it was likely to swell his finger and he wished I would take it and lay it away, and I did take it and laid it in the window in the jail, and it lay there until we taken him down yonder. And I happened to think of this ring and I went to the jail and get it and have had it in my possession until I turned it over to you (Mr. Richards). It was on his finger the night we went out there, that he stabbed himself."

CROSS EXAMINATION BY MR. RUSSELL

"I stated that I was with the Sheriff on the 23rd of December, when he and Mr. Hassell came to the County Attorney's office, and at that time I heard Mr. Thomas tell him he was under suspicion on account of the disappearance of his family—that the people were not satisfied about his story about where they were; and Mr. Hassell made up an awful pretty story about it, and he was then turned loose and went about his business. After that time, I paid him some money for some grain. I paid him for quite a bit of stuff that evening, and he had that check in his pocket when left town that evening. I don't know whether he had any other money in his pockets or not. He left town along about five or 5:30 that evening.

"Yes, sir, after that conversation he had in Mr. Thomas' office and during my dealings with him after that that evening, while he was in my presence, he appeared perfectly normal, and I couldn't see anything out of the way. Well he was just a little more nervous that day than he had been but not enough to say much about it."

RUSSELL: "You decided that he was a little nervous at that time since this other thing came up, didn't you?"

HAWKINS: "No, I noticed it in the office a little bit, not much. I just figured it was on account of his talking to the County Attorney and the Sheriff, which would naturally make a man feel a little bit bad or a little nervous.

"It would be calculated to make the ordinary man feel nervous to accuse him of something like we did him, even if he hadn't been guilty, it was ordinarily 'shoot' an ordinary man all to pieces. That is the way I figured it.

"We officers generally notice that when we make such a serious accusation as that, it generally makes the party extremely nervous, whether he committed the act or not. But I didn't notice this on Mr. Hassell any more than on anybody else would.

"Yes, I heard most of Mr. Thomas and Mr. Martin's testimony last night, in which they said that they didn't notice anything unusual about Mr. Hassell and that they only wanted his explanation because the situation was unusual and had to be cleared up; and at that time, I didn't notice anything extraordinarily nervous about him at all myself. And Mr. Hassell was permitted to go home after he had made that accusation.

"There have been times when Mr. Hassell would be more nervous than others. After he had that operation, of course, he was more nervous than usual. The physical shock, loss of blood, etc., would necessarily be calculated to cause a man some stress at such a time. I have had occasion to observe him quite frequently since he has been a prisoner, and it is a fact that he goes on and jokes and carries on conversations and talks about everything just as if he never had a worry or trouble in the world.

He talks about it and remarks, he says, 'I will get what I deserve,' or something to that effect. But he never appears to be particularly troubled about it. He talks and jokes with the doctors when they would go to dress his wounds. He asked the doctor at Plainview if he was trying to embalm him when he poured some fluid into his wounds; and he laughed and talked to everybody that he had an opportunity to talk to about the same matter, and he kept that up constantly and continuously since he has been under arrest. And he laughed and talked and joked with the photographers when they took the pictures and suggested that he get between a couple of Sheriffs and give them a reputation for having handled the biggest criminal in the State of Texas. He made that remark and laughed and joked about it."

It is interesting to note that the prosecutor and defense counsel were trying to elicit testimony that would paint Hassell in two opposite lights: either as a cunning killer with nary a worry in the world or as a psycho who was completely off his rocker.

The transcript reads to me as if Hassell were a psychopath.

The witnesses would have been forewarned not to discuss any of Hassell's past criminal activity and certainly not the allegation that he had murdered another family in California nearly a decade earlier. News stories soon after Hassell's arrest began to mention the California case, but Judge Tatum protected Hassell from any prejudicial testimony, and it's unknown if jurors read any of these accounts or heard the gossip.

RE-DIRECTION EXAMINATION BY MR. RICHARDS

"I have heard him talk a good deal, having been with him quite a lot. And I heard him talk about various lines, about his trouble, and different things, and I will say that I never noticed anything out of the way or that appeared to be irrational about his conversations."

RE-CROSS EXAMINATON BY MR. RUSSELL

"I said I saw nothing out of the way in his conversations.

RUSSELL: "It isn't irrational or unusual—I will use the word 'unusual'—for the man who is accused of killing nine people with the possibility of the electric chair staring him in the face, for him to laugh and tell folks jokes and appear not to have any concern whatsoever about it."

HAWKINS: "I don't know about that. I never saw a man that done a thing like that before."

RUSSELL: "You said you never saw anything irrational about him. Would you say an ordinary, rational man with that confronting him, and after being accused of what he was, could it be rational for him to laugh and joke about it afterwards?"

HAWKINS: "I don't know."

RUSSELL: "Based on your experience and common observation, as to how the ordinary man would act—"

HAWKINS: "You take a man if he sees and knows what he is into, he might try to pass it off that way and get by."

RUSSELL: "I am asking you from your experience and observation, measured from your own mental observation. Is it natural or rational for a man to act in this manner as you observed under these circumstances?"

HAWKINS: "I don't know what others would do. I helped handle him, and he seemed to think he was going to get a pretty good punishment. He would laugh and talk about it and he would say 'I am going to get what is coming to me.'"

RUSSELL: "You are not exactly answering the question. Maybe what you say is right, but I am asking you now, from the conduct of this defendant, when he laughs and jokes and takes on like you testify he does, and with what he is accused of doing, is that a natural or rational thing for a man to do? Just speaking about the ordinary man. I want you to answer that, yes or no."

HAWKINS: "Well I couldn't say."

The deputy just wouldn't budge on the attorney's strong push to paint Hassell as mentally unbalanced.

RUSSELL: "That is all."

RICHARDS: "That is all."

And the witness was excused. What happened next needs some context to fully understand. Skilled attorneys spend much time strategizing the "road map" of how they want the trial to flow, so that it is easily understood by jurors and will result in an appropriate verdict.

Today a coroner probably would kick off the trial to lay the foundation of the time of death, location, cause of death, and identity of the victims. The coroner would be followed on the witness stand by the first responders, who would identify the scene and identify the defendant as the alleged killer, and would describe the circumstances of the arrest.

In the case against Hassell, the prosecution decided to blow the case wide open with Hassell's dramatic and graphic confession. The impact of the confession at that precise moment would hopefully convince jurors that there was really no question about what happened in the farmhouse just before Christmas.

Murder trials always involve family members who are introduced either as spectators or witnesses. That usually happens during opening arguments, when a prosecutor points to the victims' family gathered in the front row just behind his chair and asks jurors to give them peace with a just verdict.

Prosecutor Richards chose at that time in the trial to call as witness a family member without much of an introduction. Nora Gigler was Susan and Thomas Hassell's eldest child and the sole survivor of this family annihilator. Nora Gigler's testimony had only one purpose. And it does not seem as important in the context of the entire murder spree as her possible testimony about her suspicions and visit to Farwell that summer.

Her testimony could not have taken more than a few minutes.

DIRECT EXAMINATION BY MR. RICHARDS

"My name is Mrs. Gigler, and I am Mrs. Hassell's eldest child. I am the only remaining member of the family. Aldon Hassell was my brother. He was twenty-one-years-old the 25th day of August last year.

"Yes, I recognize the ring you hand me. It is the ring that I gave to my brother Aldon for his birthday. The way I recognize it is because when I bought it, it wasn't quite large enough for him, and my mother had a piece set in it. I told her to have it done so it would be large enough for him. And you can see on this ring that it has had a piece put in. I could say that is Aldon's ring."

RUSSELL: "No questions."

RICHARDS: "I would like to offer this ring in evidence as Plaintiff's Exhibit Number Four."

(The Reporter thereupon identified the ring as Plaintiff's Exhibit Number Four).

Deputy Hawkins earlier testified Hassell gave him the ring because it was too small for his finger and probably was hurting him. Hawkins stated that he had kept it safe.

So it's clear that Hassell pulled the ring from the finger of his dead step-son before tossing the young man into the backyard pit.

Nora could have testified that George Hassell had tried to lure her to Farwell so that he could kill the last remaining Hassell child, but maybe the prosecutor thought that was too prejudicial or merely unnecessary at this point. There is no clue, however, in the trial transcript. Ferguson family history provides an insight into the case with some letters indicating that Nora had been contacted by Hassell—probably after the murders—and told that her mother had requested her to come immediately. Family stories indicate that Nora became suspicious. There is no other information regarding whether she contacted authorities in Farwell or when she was notified of the murders.

Nora's brief testimony is more intriguing for what it omits. She could have provided far more enlightenment regarding the chemistry between her mother and George Hassell and possibly the rape of her younger sister.

Maybe Prosecutor Richards thought he had sufficient evidence to convict at this point. Maybe he never fully interviewed Nora before her testimony. Maybe the Fergusons were so humiliated by the revelations in the confession that they decided to keep any family input quiet.

The prosecutor next called a witness who could nail down the events involving young Aldon Hassell's last days before he went home to where his family had been slaughtered.

"My name is G. W. Crawford, and I live in Clovis. My business is running a thresh machine generally." Threshing is the practice of separating the grain from the stalk, a part of wheat processing that dates back to farmers in biblical times. "I know the defendant, George J. Hassell, and I know his boy, Aldon; Aldon is really his step-son.

"Yes, sir, I have done threshing in this part of the country; I am threshing over here now. That is where I threshed all fall. Aldon Hassell worked for me early in December of last year. When he worked for me, I was threshing about three or five miles south of Bovina. Aldon commenced working for me, let's see—he worked for me two weeks and a half. He worked for me on up until the fourth of December. That was on Saturday. His work was oiling the separator, and I was paying him $3 a day for his work. He worked until the night of December the 4th, Saturday night, and he came home with me.

"I have two boys of my own. Aldon went over there with me and my boys in the car on that Saturday night. I think he went home with us so he could stay with the boys all night and to the picture show. I heard him say just before we left that he wanted to go to the picture show. That was Saturday night, the 4th of December.

"Well he went with us and spent the night. And Sunday morning, we got up kind of late. It was a rainy morning, and I believe it snowed a little bit. They stayed around the house and read some novels, and we had breakfast kind of late.

"So there was a boy there from where I was threshing and had been threshing for a day or two by the name of Griffith. He came over to Clovis that night, too. And Sunday morning, he came down to our house, and they all stayed around there until two or three o'clock in the afternoon. That was Sunday, the 5th of December. So I told my boy 'You get in the car and go drain the boiler at the threshing machine because we got to work Monday.' The boiler was over four miles, I believe, as well as I remember, south of Bovina. So the Griffith boy says he had to go right by Mr. Hassell's and so my boy went with him, and the Hassell boy also went with them. They took Aldon Hassell by Mr. Hassell's place. They said they got there about four or five o'clock, the best they could tell, and they left Aldon Hassell there at his home. That was Sunday, the 5th of December. That was the last I ever saw Aldon Hassell."

That date does not match the timeline provided in Hassell's confession.

"On Monday, the 6th of December, I saw the defendant George J. Hassell here in Farwell or Texico, I am not sure which side of the line it was on, and I had a talk with him at that time. Just the words I can't speak, but anyway I met him, and he told me that the boy, Aldon, had gone to Oklahoma. That is as well as I remember. That was on Monday morning, the 6th of December, I am almost sure. Anyway, when I went back to Clovis on this same day, my wife told me that Mr. Hassell had come over to my house. That was over at Clovis. And told her his boy wouldn't be with me anymore and for me to look out for some other hand. I am almost sure that was Monday morning. So when I saw Hassell, I told him I hadn't paid this boy for his week's work. And I believe I said to him, 'Could I pay you,' and he made the remark 'Yes,' that he would give him (Aldon) my check or the money, I don't remember just the words he said. So I paid him $18, which covered the week's work. I paid him by writing him a check, and I have that check here now (Hands the check to Mr. Richards). That is the check I gave George J. Hassell on December 6th. I think Mr. Hassell did the writing of that check himself, and the first endorsement on the back of it is Mr. Hassell's. I don't know whether it is his signature, but his name appears on the back of it, and it is the same name as appears on the front of the check. This is a cancelled check, and I got it from the bank with my monthly statement. The check paid Aldon Hassell up to the night of December 4th."

RICHARDS: "We would like to offer the check in evidence. Any objections?"

RUSSELL: "No."

(Thereupon the check was marked by the Reporter for identification as Plaintiff's Exhibit Number Five and hereinafter appears in evidence in words and figures as follows.)

Crawford continued with his testimony.

"I saw Mr. Hassell again after Monday the 6th. I am not positive of that date, but as well as I remember, it was the next day. I stopped at Mr. Hassell's house that day and talked to him some few minutes at the house, and I loaned him my car that day, along in the evening. He said he wanted the car to go to Clovis. Said he broke his watch—that a horse had thrown him in the stubble field. Well I had to wait to see a party here along about three o'clock in the afternoon, as well as I remember, and he told me while I was waiting for those people if I didn't mind, he would take my car and go to Clovis, and I told him to go ahead. So he left in my car and came back in about an hour and showed me his watch that he had had in the jewelry store to have fixed."

CROSS-EXAMINATION

RUSSELL: "This conversation you said you had with Mr. Hassell at the time you paid him, the $18 check. At that time, you first mentioned the fact that you hadn't paid Aldon, didn't you?"

CRAWFORD: "Just as I tell you. Just as those words came, I don't know."

RUSSELL: "You mentioned it first, did you?"

CRAWFORD: "I wouldn't say. But it seems like I did."

RUSSELL: "That is all."

(Witness excused)

This witness' testimony is rather curious.

Crawford apparently was called to pinpoint as best he could the date that Aldon could have been murdered. Authorities seemed uncertain when the others were killed, but Crawford could pin it down to early morning of December 6th. The check written to George J. Hassell and cashed by him provides a good timeline.

The poignancy of the thresher's testimony about Aldon working hard for a week and then enjoying a Saturday night movie with some buddies struck me as so tragic. He was working to bring in extra money for his large family, only to return home to find his mother and siblings gone, then he enjoyed his last meal with a step-father who had stuffed his mother's and siblings' bodies in a backyard pit.

If this was not ghoulish enough, reading that Hassell so callously cashed the check and pocketed Aldon's hard-earned money struck me as profoundly sad. And that might explain why the defense counsel wanted to blunt some of the emotion by making it as clear as possible that Hassell did not ask for the money first; it was Crawford who offered to pay the debt.

When you are grasping at straws to save a killer, I guess you take any straw you can find.

Another prosecution witness testified about the auction at Hassell's place.

"My name is R. F. Lloyd, and I live four and one-half miles southeast of Bovina with my father. My father's name is W. M. Lloyd.

"I am twenty-one-years-old; I was twenty-one the 29th of July.

"Yes, sir, I remember being present at the Hassell place east of Farwell at a public sale on the 22nd of December. I was there most of the day, and I think they sold most everything that there was around there. I bought a shot gun myself. It was just a single barreled shot gun, twelve gauge. It will only shoot two shells at a time. I paid either $9 or $9.50 for it. It was just offered for sale, and I bid on it.

"The gun you hand me is the gun I bought at the sale and about which I have been testifying. It is not loaded now; yes, I am sure it isn't. It carries the shells in here. One goes in the barrel, and one goes down in here (illustrating). I don't know what sort of gun you would call it. I don't notice any name on it."

RICHARDS: "We will offer the gun in evidence."

RUSSELL: "No objection."

RICHARDS: "He (the witness) can withdraw it after we are through. I would like to have the gentlemen of the jury to see it. That is all."

(Thereupon the gun was marked by the Reporter for identification as Plaintiff's Exhibit Number Six.)

CROSS EXAMINATION

WITNESS: "You ask me how long I had known Aldon Hassell. Well Mr. Crawford threshed over at our place, and Aldon was working for him is all I knew.

"I don't know whether they sold all of the stuff at the sale or not, but I noticed them selling numerous things. They sold dishes, clothing, and the ordinary knick knacks that the ordinary family would accumulate. All such things were being sold, and Mr. Hassell was around there conducting the sale; he was bringing out things and talking some. He talked and acted just like an ordinary man would, and I couldn't see anything unusual about him at all. And he would bring those things out and take them over to the auctioneer. He would tell about the things to be sold, etc., and kept that course of action up all the time as far as I could see."

With that Lloyd was excused.

Those in the jury box and those spectators inside the courtroom likely greatly anticipated the testimony of the tall graying man seated near the front of the courtroom. Sure, Hassell's confession was sensational, but it was read by an attorney and not by Hassell himself. Had this man been coached by the prosecutor to be brief and stick to only answering the carefully crafted questions? What was he going to say? He was a witness everybody wanted to hear.

"My name is P. M. Ferguson, and I live in Colorado, about thirty miles beyond Springfield.

RICHARDS: "What relation were you to …"

FERGUSON: (interrupting) "She is my daughter."

RICHARDS: "How is that?"

FERGUSON: "She is my daughter."

That exchange hints of some agitation between the prosecutor and Pleasant. Was he still upset about not being notified of the murders? Maybe he was just angry about being in the courtroom facing George Hassell.

"I have been here in Farwell—well we come down as soon as we saw about this in the paper; about the latter days of December.

"George J. Hassell was her second husband; his brother was her first husband. His name was Tom, 'T. V.' All I know about his death is what my daughter wrote to me. I wasn't there myself."

I find this passage curious in that he discusses the death of Thomas Hassell. Rumors were flying in Farwell about the possibility that George had killed his brother. Pleasant kept any suspicions to himself.

"My daughter, Mrs. Hassell, had eight living children (he forgets Sammie); they were children by T. V. Hassell and were George J. Hassell's step-children.

"I can't recall the date that this defendant and Mrs. Hassell were married, but it was a couple of months after his brother got killed; it has been about two years ago.

"I have been out to the Hassell place east of town three times since I have been here and noticed around the premises three different places where something had been burned, and I scratched into these places and investigated them to see if I could find any mark or anything by which I could identify my daughter. In one of the places, I found some pearl buttons and some hair pins. But the pearl buttons had been in such a hot fire, you couldn't pick them up because they would crumble to nothing. Then there was a little place, kind of a little hole in the ground where the fire didn't reach very much, where I found a little piece of goods with a big button on it, and it was a piece off of a brown cloak. I also found a small piece of a quilt with blood on it, and under that was a tick and some feathers, and you could see where some oil had been poured on it. The larger piece I mentioned had some blood on it; it didn't hardly look like blood, but evidently it was. But it was all in ashes, and I wouldn't have even found this if it hadn't been for that little hole in the ground so the fire didn't reach it.

"I said I had been out to the place three times. The first time I was there, I went through the house. It was at night, and I was hurt so bad that I couldn't make much of an examination."

Pleasant Ferguson testified for about five minutes, at best, and the prosecutor ended his questioning.

Now the defense attorney had the chore to either cross-examine Pleasant or not to ask any questions. Not asking at least one question would only serve to underline Pleasant's last comment.

CROSS-EXAMINATION

Russell apparently asked a simple question about the children.

"I said my daughter married this defendant's brother first, and these children were the children by her first husband, and this defendant's step-children, and of course, would have been his nieces and nephews."

And that was Pleasant's entire testimony.

The prosecution then called another family member, Aunt Susie's older brother John.

"My name is Ferguson, and my initials are J. V. I live in Grey, Oklahoma and am a farmer."

Firm, tough, right to the point. This witness could seal the deal against his brother-in-law.

"I am Mrs. Hassell's brother.

"I have been in Farwell about two weeks and have been out to the Hassell place once during that time.

"When my sister, Susie Hassell, lived with her first husband, they lived in Blair, Oklahoma. Her husband died about July 1924. He was a farmer. He had started a crop for 1924 but died before the crop was finished. He died in July. That 1924 crop was principally cotton. I don't remember the exact number of bales it made but something like forty-five to forty-eight bales was my understanding. Cotton was a pretty good price that fall, fair price anyway.

"Mrs. Hassell's first husband tried to specialize in raising good stuff in the way of good turkeys, hogs, and so forth. I understood that they took some prizes on some of their cotton. It was a variety of half and half cotton, I understood, that they took the premium on.

"Mrs. Hassell collected eleven hundred dollars on the life of her first husband."

CROSS-EXAMINATION

"When my sister's first husband died, Mrs. Hassell sent me a telegram that he died, and I went to her assistance the day I received the telegram. We were harvesting at the time. The message came on the Fourth of July, and that is the day I left to go help my sister arrange things, although most of the arrangements had been made by the time I got there.

"Judge Hendricks paid the funeral expenses, and Mrs. Hassell reimbursed him out of the insurance. He is the man who owned the land on which she lived at that time. He advanced the immediate expenses, such as the hospital bill and the undertaker, and was repaid later out of the insurance.

"Half of all the crop went to the land owner, so there was something like twenty-four bales of cotton left for my sister.

"I recall a visit George J. Hassell and his wife, my sister, made at our place a little over a year ago. They made two visits, and I will tell the jury about the last one, the last time I saw George J. Hassell. The occasion was a family reunion, and the majority of the family was to be together. Something came up that night that Mr. Hassell took exception to, and he really got pretty sore. In other words, he didn't let his family sleep in the house and he taken them all outside. I didn't go outside and don't know what he said out there. No, sir, he didn't abuse the Ferguson family. But the next morning he got up raving some more, and I finally got all of it I could stand, so I just says to him 'Mr. Hassell, you have said enough now, and I don't want another word out of you,' and he never returned another word to me."

RE-DIRECT EXAMINATION

PROSECUTOR: "You have seen other men get mad."

FERGUSON: "Yes."

PROSECUTOR: "A good many of them?"

FERGUSON: "Yes."

DEFENSE COUNSEL: "We object to that—the mere fact that he has seen other men get mad."

JUDGE: "Over-rule that."

DEFENSE COUNSEL: "That is in rebuttal."

JUDGE: "Over-ruled."

DEFENSE COUNSEL: "Note our exception."

PROSECUTOR: "That's all."

And John Ferguson was excused after giving some background on Thomas Hassell's death and a family reunion in which George Hassell's temper became a big problem. Perhaps Hassell's attorney had no clue what John was going to discuss, but the testimony certainly didn't improve Hassell's standing.

What was the argument about? One clue might have been in Hassell's confession about his rape of Maudie. Could the step-daughter he was molesting have shared her secret with her cousins? Did Maudie tell my mother at that reunion about what her step-father had done to her? My mother was very innocent and protected, and I wonder whether she learned this after the murders. If Maudie did confide in my mom, I cannot imagine Mom not telling my grandmother about that secret and Grandmother alerting her older sister Susan.

The prosecution apparently was content to rely on Hassell's confession and focus on the murder of Aldon.

The prosecutor's questions seem to focus on Hassell's mental status. Yes, he looks normal. Yes, he killed a lot of people. Yes, he tried to commit suicide and said some pretty strange things, but he seemed pretty normal to the people with whom he dealt in the days following the Christmas murders. That seems to sum up testimony of witnesses so far.

The next prosecution witness, whose testimony no doubt came in the early evening, would buttress the prosecution's contention that George J. Hassell wasn't crazy.

"My name is Doctor E. L. Smith. I live in Clovis, New Mexico and am connected with the Baptist Sanitarium at Clovis. My business is medicine and surgery. I am a graduate of an accredited school of medicine and surgery and hold a diploma from the Saint Louis University. I am what you call a regular practitioner and have been practicing medicine for about twenty-five years and am now regularly engaged in the practice of medicine and surgery.

"I know the defendant here, George J. Hassell. I had occasion to see him about the morning of December 24th of last year in the operating room of the Baptist Sanitarium at Clovis, New Mexico and made an examination of him at that time. He had a wound on his left wrist and three wounds in his body. I made an examination and performed an operation on him at that time. Two of his wounds were about a half inch deep, and the other penetrated the abdominal cavity, just below the rib. I treated him for the wounds. The 'omentum' is an apron shape arrangement that sort of covers over the intestines, and that was protruding out of this one deep stab wound. I made an incision about four inches and took part of this 'omentum' off and put the other back and took care of him the best I could.

"Yes, sir, I regarded that as a serious wound, and I operated on him there at the sanitarium. They took him away that night, I believe, after he had been under my care about a day at the sanitarium. After that, however, I saw him on the 24th, 25th, 26th, 27th, and 28th here at Farwell. Then I saw him again the 6th at Muleshoe.

"I talked with him some during the time I was treating and waiting on him and observed his demeanor during that time and noted his method of talking and expressing himself and his reasoning. I have had some experience in observing and studying the mental activities of people."

DEFENSE COUNSEL: "I am going to interpose an objection now, Doctor. I am anticipating what the District Attorney is driving at, and until he qualifies the doctor as an expert, I will object to any testimony as to the mental condition of this defendant."

(Witness continuing) "I have had just the ordinary experience that comes to the average doctor, so far as observing mental troubles is concerned. Such experience covers a period of about twenty-five years. Yes, I studied those troubles some while in school and for about twenty-five years during general practice."

PROSECUTOR: "I will ask you whether or not from your experience and observation in that line you are capable of passing intelligent judgment on the mental condition of a man."

DOCTOR: "That would be a hard question to answer because I haven't specialized in that."

PROSECUTOR: "Well I will ask you individually whether you think you are capable of passing judgment in that respect."

JUDGE: "Objection sustained."

PROSECUTOR: "You say you have treated people for that for some twenty-five years. State to the jury what you observed with reference to this man's conversation; that is as to whether or not it was coherent and reasoned from cause to effect and so on."

DEFENSE COUNSEL: "We object to that as a conclusion and opinion."

PROSECUTOR: "I am asking for the facts—not a conclusion."

JUDGE: "Over-ruled."

DEFENSE COUNSEL: "Note our objection."

DOCTOR: "Yes, he talked rational to me, coherent. One hundred percent good patient."

PROSECUTOR: "Did you notice anything about his conversation or conduct during the time he was under your care that appeared to you, as a physician and surgeon, to be irrational and abnormal?"

DEFENSE COUNSEL: "We object to that as a conclusion of the witness; he is not qualified."

JUDGE: "Over-ruled."

DEFENSE COUNSEL: "Note our exception."

DOCTOR: "No, he didn't. Mr. Hassell talked of many different things, some of his experiences, talked of his boyhood days, and of his trouble in California, the trouble he had here, something about his life being checkered, some of the things he had to combat, etc. He said that in his opinion, wine and women had caused his trouble."

DEFENSE COUNSEL: "We object to that. The defendant was under arrest at the time."

JUDGE: "Where was the defendant at that time?"

DOCTOR: "Here in the jail."

JUDGE: "Sustain the objection; gentlemen, you will not consider that."

PROSECUTOR: "What statement did he make to you along that line while he was in the sanitarium at Clovis?"

DEFENSE COUNSEL: "We object to that because he confessed before he was carried to Clovis, and the sheriff and Deputy and County Attorney was standing there watching the operation."

JUDGE: "Over-ruled."

PROSECUTOR: "No, sir, no arrest has been shown yet."

DEFENSE COUNSEL: "Well we except of course."

PROSECUTOR: "Go ahead, Doctor, and state what his conversation was over in the sanitarium that day."

DOCTOR: "Well I had no conversation with him in the sanitarium that day. I don't recall anything that I said to him.

PROSECUTOR: "Take the witness."

CROSS-EXAMINATION BY MR. RUSSELL

"Mr. Hassell, while my patient nearly always seem cheerful, not always but nearly always (sic). He and I had discussions and conversations, and on one occasion, he told me he was going to live 'for my reputation.' He talked freely to me."

RUSSELL: "And he talked like an ordinary man that didn't have any particular troubles at all."

WITNESS: "No, I wouldn't say that all the time. Sometimes he would express concern. Sometimes he seemed to be worried about something. The last time I saw him here in jail, he did, but generally speaking, he didn't seem to be worried about anything, and he would talk and laugh with me generally, and he was inclined to joke."

RUSSELL: "And when he would talk about this checkered career, he would do it in a casual way as an ordinary man would talk about an ordinary experience."

WITNESS: "Sometimes he did and sometimes he didn't."

RUSSELL: "What do you mean by that?"

WITNESS: "Sometimes he showed some feeling."

RUSSELL: "What do you mean by feeling?"

WITNESS: "For instance tears came to his eyes and his lips quivered the last time I talked with him in jail.

"At that time, he was discussing some phase of this affair, which he is accused of now. Just once before that, I thought he showed a little feeling."

RUSSELL: "That was while you were dressing his wounds?"

WITNESS: "No, sir, after I had finished."

RUSSELL: "Did you make a habit of sitting and talking with him after you had dressed his wounds?"

WITNESS: "I was only over here four times and . . ."

RUSSELL: (interrupting) "Doctor, as a matter of fact, the time you say you saw tears coming into his eyes was when you were pulling some adhesive tape off of his wounds, wasn't it?"

WITNESS: "No, sir, it was, as I said, a while ago.

"Ordinarily he talked to me like a fellow who had no concern whatever about anything.

"I also dressed his wounds in Muleshoe, and at that time, he said something about the doctor at Plainview trying to embalm him, by pouring some fluid on his wounds, and he seemed to have a big time about that and talked like a man that didn't have a care in the world.

"Yes, sir, I said I have had twenty-five years of experience and had had occasion, of course, to observe the ordinary human conduct, conduct of people who are sick and in trouble and distress, and as a matter of fact, mental conditions will effect a person physically to a considerable extent. People who are worried and troubled about things will usually largely make up the doctor's bunch of patients, to some extent at least. And the doctor, necessarily to be a good doctor, has got to look into the history of the patient and find out some things about his or her mental condition in order to make a proper diagnosis.

"When people are in trouble or have had occasion to be accused of a crime, I have observed that most ordinary people become worried about it. Of course they may take it in different ways, but in the majority of cases, you are right when you say that they would be worried over a situation like that, and the majority of people who are accused of having committed a serious crime will show a great deal of mental stress. And I say that is the usual and ordinary mental attitude of the person who is in trouble."

WITNESS EXCUSED

Jurors were hearing testimony that Hassell was not acting like a normal guy who is suddenly accused of a heinous murder spree and thrust into the spotlight of public opinion. But did that make him insane? Defense attorney Russell had done his best to show jurors that Hassell just wasn't acting rationally after the crimes. "Normal" people don't joke and chatter at times of great stress, such as being accused of capital murder. Was Russell grasping at straws at this point?

The next witness discussed Hassell's financial transactions after the murders occurred.

"My name is F. U. McCutcheon, and I am in the banking business, being connected with the Security State Bank of Farwell.

"I know the defendant, George J. Hassell; he was a customer of my bank and had been a customer practically one year.

"I recall the incident of his having a sale on the Hassell place about the 22nd of December. Some two or three weeks prior to the sale, Mr. Hassell made arrangements with me about handling notes in connection with that sale. He came in and told me that he was going to have a sale and wanted to know if I would handle the paper on the sale. I told him I would up to some four or five hundred dollars.

"After the sale, the proceeds were deposited in my bank, which amounted to about $1,000 in cash. There had already been one deposit of $600 from the sale of the wheat, which would make his deposits in the bank total a little better that $1,600. He had a total deposit of somewhere in the neighborhood of $1,800.

"The notes on the proceeds of the sale were never placed with the bank. They were left with the Clerk, and some of them notes had never been drawn up. The notes were never turned over to me. I know what the notes would amount to only from a statement from Mr. Hassell. He said the notes would run a little better than what he anticipated, a little more than $500.

"No, sir, he did not go ahead and cash those notes with me; in order to do that, he would've had to bring them down and endorsed them, and only the ones I approved would have been taken. That would have been necessary before I would have taken them and given him any money on them. He hadn't done that on the night of the 23rd and he hasn't done it to date. I understand some of the notes have never been made yet.

"Mr. Hassell was good to pay his debts. He was the first man who paid me his notes this year. Sure, I observed his methods of doing business, and I talked with him as much as I do the ordinary customer at the bank I presume. We considered him a very reliable farmer and a very attentive man to business and systematic in his work and business-like in his methods, up until the 23rd of December. I never noticed anything abnormal about his methods or conduct. He was in to see me even on the 23rd of December, and his actions and conduct were all right, just about the same as always."

CROSS-EXAMINATION BY MR. RUSSELL

"Mr. Overstreet has those notes, I presume. Mr. Overstreet works for the Capitol Syndicate office—Judge Hamlin's office.

"I said I never noticed any difference in the conduct, talk, or actions of Mr. Hassell after the first day of December, clear on up to the 23rd. He was in the bank on the 23rd, and I have since learned that he had a talk with the County Attorney and Sheriff on that day about the disappearance of his family. I didn't know that, however, at the time he was in the bank, he appeared to be perfectly normal, no excitement or apparent nervousness so far as I observed."

RE-DIRECT EXAMINATION BY MR. RICHARDS

"If the Sheriff or any officers made any inquiry of me about his bank (Mr. Hassell's) account on through 23rd of December, I don't recall it. There is another man who works in the bank by the name of Hood.

"If Mr. Hassell had come into my bank late in the evening of the 23rd and wanted to cash a check for that amount of his deposit in the bank, I would have paid him the money."

RICHARDS: "What else could you have done?"

WITNESS: "Well, after having heard the rumors that I heard, I would have more than likely called an officer."

RICHARDS: "Of course you would have had to pay the money if he had presented a check. But you say you would have notified the officers. All right, that is all."

WITNESS EXCUSED

What did Hassell intend to do? High tail it out of town after the holidays? From the testimony, it seems the prosecutor wanted to suggest that Hassell's disappearance from the scene of the crime had been imminent.

The prosecution was not going to give up hammering the jury with testimony that Hassell showed signs of a guilty conscience. In Farwell they were hard-pressed to understand the mind of a psychopath.

The next witness, the wife of the most important man in town, was recalled to the witness stand. Kate Hamlin was the Hassells' landlord, who kept a close watch on her tenant farmers.

KATE HAMLIN: "I testified yesterday about seeing Mr. Hassell at one time along after the first of December and asking him if he had any trouble with his family. That was probably, let's see—that was sometime the first week in December, I think, along about that time. I had asked him before that about his family. This time I think we were talking possibly about the possibility of him continuing farming there. He had been giving me his idea of what he had intended to do. Anyway I looked at him sharply and asked him if he had been having trouble with his family, and it seemed to startle him. He hesitated before he answered me and didn't look me in the face for a little bit. He looked off—rather down—before he answered me. He made no reply, but he looked back and rather gave the impression that he had (had trouble with his family). I won't say that he quite said yes, but he gave me the impression that he had. He was nervous at that time.

"After that time, I was present at the sale on the 23rd of December and I noticed him on that day when he appeared to be nervous. Once I remember that in the morning about that time the fruit was being sold, I offered to help him. He couldn't hand it to the Clerk fast enough and he told me he had two boys hired and that they were out in the crowd talking and not attending to their business and that he couldn't get it done by himself. It was at that time that I noticed he was upset and seemed to be very nervous. And at the time he told me that, I noticed that his eyes filled with tears.

"Then I noticed the day he was at my table eating dinner, the day I asked him what scratched his face and hands, and I noticed when he answered me his eyes filled with tears, and that was possibly the only sign of nervousness.

"And Mr. Richards, I think Mr. Hassell showed nervousness the day I asked him about the time of the sale. I was looking at one of the handbills, and I looked at him and I says, 'Mr. Hassell, what is Mrs. Hassell going to say to you about selling all of that stuff?' And I think he was pretty nervous over that. He did quite a bit of fidgeting, although he answered me rather promptly. At the same time, I saw that it disturbed him. In reply to that, he said 'Oh, nothing; she told me to.' This occurred possibly the day before the sale. I was looking at one of the lists of stuff he had to sell. It was either the morning of the sale or the day before; I don't remember having any conversation with him until he began the sale. At any rate, I thought he was unusually nervous at that time. There was no other times that I recall right now of having seen him in a nervous condition."

CROSS-EXAMINATION BY MR. RUSSELL

"It must have been about the first week in December that I first spoke to Mr. Hassell rather sharply about his family and asked if he had had trouble. Well that could possibly have been the second week in December. I am not certain about that. It was all about the time I found the family gone. I wasn't worried about his family all during that time, no. When he told me they were in Shallowater, I thought nothing about it. But along about the time I asked this question, I had begun to have my suspicions, and I began talking to Judge Hamlin about it; he didn't talk to me."

RUSSELL: "But the idea that you were intending to convey to him when you asked about his family, or if he had had trouble with his family, at that time you had something in your mind that there might be some foul play."

WITNESS: "I thought of the possibilities all right, but I hadn't made up my mind to it yet."

RUSSELL: "But the idea you were trying to convey was to get some truth about his family."

WITNESS: "Well possibly."

RUSSELL: "And of course, it was afterwards discovered what had become of his family."

WITNESS: "Certainly. Why yes, I talked to the District Attorney this morning. No, sir, he hasn't explained why he didn't ask me these questions last night when I was on the stand."

WITNEESS EXCUSED

After hearing from eighteen prosecution witnesses, Prosecutor Richards was nearing the end of his case and chose to call as his last witness somebody whose testimony was, well, anti-climactic.

It is unknown why Richards would choose to throw this morsel into the proverbial pot for the jury to chew on, but it seemed to add some proof that Hassell was just plain weird.

"My name is D. O. Fayville, and my business is running the drug store in Texico.

"I know the defendant, George J. Hassell, by sight. I recall his coming into my place of business sometime in December and returning some merchandise he had bought. I can't remember the date, but it was a couple days before his sale.

"The package you hand me looks like the item that he returned. It is Wine of Cardui. The paper that is wrapped around it is a bill of sale, and that sale bill was wrapped around it when he returned it to me.

"This Wine of Cardui is a women's tonic. As far as I know, this carton correctly sets forth what it should be used for and that is what it is sold for.

"I should think there has been just a little bit used out of that bottle. When Mr. Hassell brought the bottle back to me, he told me that the medicine didn't taste like that—that his wife and daughter tasted it and said it didn't taste like the medicine they had taken before, and he asked me to take it back. He said it wasn't right—something wrong with it, and he wanted me to take it back. He just brought it back for credit; he hadn't paid for it. The price was $1.

"I don't know just when this happened, but it would be just a couple of days I should say, or three days, before the sale, close to the date of the sale, and the sale was on the 22nd of December, I believe."

CROSS EXAMINATION BY MR. RUSSELL

"I recall, and my books show, when he bought that medicine. I don't recall it myself, but my books show it, and I forgot to look that up. I have the charge slip yet. I assume it was before the first of December 1926, or about the first of December, but I would have to look it up to tell you for sure."

PROSECUTOR: "I can give you the date; it was November 28th."

RUSSELL: "That is all right."

WITNESS: "He kept that medicine until about a day or two before the sale and then brought it back to me and asked for credit. In my experience as a druggist, I have seen that happen before. I wouldn't give you any specific cases or medicine or date, but it has happened before that medicines have been returned with the explanation that it didn't do what it was supposed to, or what they expected of it, or that something was wrong with it. However, I will say that it is a very unusual occurrence."

WITNESS EXCUSED

PROSECUTOR: “The State will rest.”

The Defense

JUDGE: "We will adjourn until 1:30 this afternoon."

There remained some discrepancies and confusion over the exact time of the deaths. A school superintendent next testified for the defense about the Hassell children's school attendance.

COURT REPORTER: "Thereupon, at the hour of 12 o'clock noon, a recess was had in the hearing of the above numbered and entitled cause until the hour of 1:30 P.M. of the same day, at which time the following proceedings were had as follows to wit:"

"My name is F. W. Sawyer, and I am Superintendent of the Public Schools of Farwell, Texas. I have occupied that position since September 1926.

"I was acquainted with the Hassell children; they attended the public school here, and I have a record of their attendance. Personally I don't remember, but my records show the last day that each one of them attended. The record shows that Davis was there December 1st, and after that, he is shown absent. He was there December 1st and December 2nd, 3rd, 4th, and so forth he was marked absent until he was withdrawn."

Neither defense nor prosecutor questions who "Davis" is, but the witness probably meant David.

"I had occasion to see Mr. Hassell along about the early part of December; he came to my office and stated that his purpose was to return the books the children had to the state. I think he returned all of their books but three. He returned, I guess, twenty books. We had a conversation together at that time. I had not been previously acquainted with Mr. Hassell, and that was the first time I had ever seen him that I know of.

"No, sir, I did not notice anything extraordinary in his demeanor that morning. He appeared perfectly normal and showed no signs of excitement.

"I have seen Mr. Hassell since that date and had a conversation with him. That was last Sunday at Hereford. I had been wanting to make a study of him, sociological, psychological, and physiological, and the Sheriff gave us permission. Professor J. L. Duflock from Canyon was with me at the time, also Sheriff Martin.

"We went down to the jail, and they let us in, and we introduced ourselves, rather Mr. Martin did, in a rather informal way and we went to swapping jokes a while and then sat down and told him our purpose, and he (Mr. Hassell) volunteered to give us any information that would be of any benefit in our study. I think we were with the defendant at least five hours, and during all of that time, he was laughing and joking and in perfectly good humor, and so far as I could tell he wasn't worried at all; he showed no signs of emotion."

The most interesting part of this is that Hassell talked either without the permission of his attorney or was oblivious to the possibility of self-incrimination, many years later spelled out in the Miranda warning every arrested person is supposed to be given before any interrogation. Journalists, even at the time of these murders, routinely call the jail to try to reach the defendant and ask if he would like to tell "his side of the story."

"Well we first took up the history of his life, trying to understand his heredity and environment, and traced all on down—the history of his life until the commission of the crime out here. We didn't ask about the crime with which he is now charged; we didn't want to know about that; it wasn't our purpose. Neither did he discuss the commission of any other crime with us.

"He showed no emotion all the while he was detailing what we wanted to know. This particular crime was mentioned, but that is about all.

"Well we brought up his philosophy of life—what life is—what death is—and eternity. We traced down to some extent his ideas along those lines and found his ideas rather peculiar.

"Having gone through with that, we started taking up the social influences that had molded his life, and of course, that was about as much facts as we could get in the case. We did make some measurements of his head. I think we have about twenty measurements of his head, something like that; I won't be sure as to the number, but there was a good many.

"And of course, we studied him psychologically and sociologically. That was our main purpose in making the study that time.

"Nobody suggested to us that we do this or that we come to Hereford. That idea originated with myself, and I asked the professor from Canyon to aid me. Nobody on the part of the defense suggested any of that to me, and I didn't know that I would be called on to testify until a few hours ago. You haven't discussed it with me until just a few moments before I came on the stand.

"Mr. Hassell's ideas of eternity and so forth were rather peculiar to me.

"I am a graduate of the West Texas State Teacher's College and the University of Oklahoma. On my Bachelor's Degree, I majored in sociology and that, of course, is the field of criminology. And on my Master's Degree, I minored in that. So you see I have given those matters considerable study and thought, and this struck me as being an interesting case for study. This is my first study of this kind, but I have had occasion to observe the general run of men and women and children in the course of my teaching experience."

DEFENSE COUNSEL: "I don't know what your answer will be to this question because I never asked you. I am just trying to get some information. Could you tell from your examination and from your discussion of that five-hour intercourse you had with the defendant, as to anything about his peculiar brain formation wherein his emotional part of it may have become dormant or atrophied or diseased or anything about that condition? If you understand that question. I don't know whether I do myself or not—but perhaps you know what I am trying to say."

WITNESS: "The question is a little involved, but I will answer it negatively. I could not tell. I couldn't qualify as an expert.

"I wouldn't feel like from my examination of this defendant that I have sufficient information of this defendant, that I have sufficient information to make statement positively yes or no. I will say that I do not know."

More recently scientists have been examining the brains of serial killers with their permission—doing post-mortem examinations in an effort to understand why some people kill.

Scientists have found abnormalities in certain brain structures in some serial killers.

CROSS-EXAMINATION BY MR. RICHARDS

"Yes. I stated that my object was to make a study of Mr. Hassell sociologically and psychologically. We were trying to get at the causes that might have led up to this crime—the causes as found in heredity and environment and social influences that might have been around him.

"I said I had studied quite a bit along those lines and that we talked with this defendant in Hereford last Sunday, something like five hours at least. Necessarily in order to form any idea of what might have led up to this crime, we would have to inquire of his past life and what crimes might have been committed in his past life; however, we didn't inquire as to any crimes he had committed, except minor ones. He told us about little petty offenses that he had committed.

RICHARDS: "Well is it or not a fact, Professor, that the continued commission of crimes will after a while get a man's conscience into such a condition that a major crime would not show so much on his countenance? Is that true or not?"

WITNESS: "Well I don't know. The tendency should certainly be in that direction, or it seems to me it should. If he commits two crimes, it would have a tendency to harden him a lot more, or seems to me. And the more crimes he commits, the harder his conscience will get. I don't know, but it would be my opinion that a man could get so he could commit a crime and never show it on his face.

"Mr. Hassell talked intelligently to us."

RICHARDS: "State whether or not he would in his conversation reason from cause to effect, so to speak."

WITNESS: "Well we didn't approach him much that way. Most of our data was historical. Yes, I can tell when a man reasons from cause to effect, and I will say that I could detect that he did reason from cause to effect."

RICHARDS: "Well that is the act of a sane man, isn't it?"

WITNESS: "Probably I will have to back up a bit and state that that was pertaining to his religious philosophy where he reasoned from cause to effect."

RICHARDS: "Did he do it in any other sphere?"

WITNESS: "Probably he did, but I didn't observe it. I only observed it in his religious atmosphere, where he reasoned from cause to effect, and that reasoning was very intelligent."

RICHARDS: "Now I will ask you this question: you seem to have made a study along that line. Was the act of reasoning from cause to effect the act of a sane man or an insane man?"

WITNESS: "It is the act of a sane man.

"We talked with Mr. Hassell something like five hours.

"Now going back to the time Mr. Hassell returned the school books. At that time, he told me that his folks had gone to Oklahoma and he said the children were in school there, in reply to my question as to whether or not they were. I had about a five minutes conversation with him at that time, and he talked intelligently.

"I said David was at school the first day of December. The other children were not there the 1st of December. David was the only one of the children there on the December 1st, according to the records; I don't know personally."

RE-DIRECT EXAMINATION BY MR. RUSSELL

RUSSELL: "The District Attorney asked you considerably with reference to petty offenses leading up to graver offenses. Now from your study of criminology, or whatever you call it, is it not a fact that crimes committed against property, such as theft or embezzlement or any other crimes, as we term it in law, committed against property, have absolutely no relation to crimes of violence? Those are two separate and distinct mental characteristics, aren't they?"

WITNESS: "I cannot say that I could answer that question yes or no because I don't know."

RUSSELL: "Judging from your study of course, along these lines and your observations, perhaps. I don't know that you had any particular observations, but from studying cases, you find that it is seldom that the crimes of violence are directly related to crimes against property, except insofar as highway robbery and similar crimes are concerned."

WITNESS: "I have not seen cases both ways, Judge."

RUSSELL: "Usually we will find the petty thief and the embezzler and the forger and the counterfeiter and crimes of that character—they usually are opposed to crimes of violence, and that character and class of people would be as far from committing murder as the ordinary man could be."

WITNESS: "I know there are such criminals as that."

RUSSELL: "And the crimes of violence connected with crimes against property are cases where the highway-man starts out with a gun for the purpose of holding up somebody—for the purpose of robbery, even if it is necessary to take somebody's life. But you have in your mind, of course, a well-defined idea of the meaning of the word 'murder,' and a highway-man is not necessarily a murderer but does that for the purpose of effecting the crime of robbery. It is a rare thing that you hear of a highway-man shooting a victim. He usually undertakes to rob him without that."

WITNESS: "Yes."

RUSSELL: "It is a fact, isn't it, that this alleged criminal, or any other criminal, commences with a series of petty crimes, like deserting from the Army and Navy, but that wouldn't necessarily show any connection with the crime of murder and if he becomes more hardened. "

RICHARDS: (interrupting): "I believe I will object to the attorney lecturing the witness."

JUDGE: "I will sustain the objection as to it being leading."

RUSSELL: "The only thing I was getting at—I want to know—There may not be any direct connection between petty crimes and crimes of violence such as murder."

WITNESS: "It is possible there may not be any connection between them.

"I said that in only one instance I observed the defendant reasoning from cause to effect during our five-hour conversation over at Hereford, and that was on the subject of theology, and he arrived at conclusions rather peculiar to me; although I have heard the same theory advanced by others in somewhat the same way. It was a slight deviation, however, from any theory I have previously heard."

RE-CROSS-EXAMINATION BY MR. RICHARDS

WITNESS: "I said I only observed one instance where Mr. Hassell reasoned from cause to effect, and that was in the realm of religion. I would not say that he never so reasoned in any other realms. He may have and I didn't notice."

RICHARDS: "Now, Professor, one other thing. I don't know as I got just what I was driving at, but maybe I can find out. Is it or not a fact that any crime, big or little, against property or persons, if it is morally wrong, would have its effect on the conscience?"

WITNESS: "If it is morally wrong, it certainly must have."

RE-DIRECT EXAMINATION BY MR. RUSSELL

RUSSELL: "It would have some effect on his conscience, assuming that he had a conscience in the first place to be effected (sic)."

WITNESS: "Yes, sir, he certainly must have something there to have an effect on."

RUSSELL: "Well, Professor, this so-called conscience of ours is nothing in the world but a mental attitude, is it?"

WITNESS: "That is so, as far as I know."

RUSSELL: "And a fellow must have a sense of right and wrong before he can have a conscience."

WITNESS: "Absolutely."

RUSSELL: "And if there is something wrong with that part of his mind that differentiates between right and wrong, then we will have to say that particular person has no conscience."

WITNESS: "Well I don't know as you would necessarily have to say he would have no conscience."

RUSSELL: "If he cannot distinguish between right and wrong, he couldn't have no conscience."

WITNESS: "If he cannot."

RUSSELL: "Yes, sir. And have you not known cases or perhaps read about them and studied them in which a person would be especially bright, we will say, along most lines, and in one particular subject be just the opposite? Practically insane?"

WITNESS: "Well I have known of geniuses along one line, and in another line, he might be a 'blank.'"

RUSSELL: "Practically an imbecile so far as another line is concerned."

WITNESS: "Yes."

RUSSELL: "That is there is a certain part of the brain that causes that of course."

WITNESS: "Well psychology tells us that."

RUSSELL: "That is what we are getting at, and I am going on the theory that there is absolutely nothing to any man except his brain, so far as his conduct is concerned. When he ceases to have a brain, he is nothing but a piece of flesh. It is a man's brain; outside of that, he is no man."

WITNESS: "Yes."

RUSSELL: "Well you say you have heard of instances where a party might be a genius in one line and a blank in another."

WITNESS: "Yes."

RUSSELL: "Necessarily then I assume that condition of affairs could happen to a man in any particular line."

WITNESS: "I should think so."

RUSSELL: "A man's moral sense of right and wrong might not be developed, and yet he might be pretty fairly developed along other lines. That could happen, couldn't it?"

WITNESS: "I think so."

RUSSELL: "That is all."

RE-CROSS EXAMINATION BY MR. RICHARDS

RICHARDS: "Where is the center of emotion in a person, Professor?"

WITNESS: "Well you are asking me a question now that is just a matter of speculation on my part or anybody else's. But I should say it is certainly in the brain—the brain cells."

RICHARDS: "What about the heart as the center of emotion?"

WITNESS: "You mean the physical heart?"

RICHARDS: "Yes."

WITNESS: "Personally I don't [know if] it has anything to do with it."

RICHARDS: "You think emotion originates in the brain?"

WITNESS: "Yes."

RICHARDS: "Without reference to the heart."

WITNESS: "Yes, sir."

RICHARDS: "All right, that is all."

RE-DIRECT EXAMINATION BY MR. RUSSELL

RUSSELL: "The heart is nothing but a muscular organ."

WITNESS: "That is all it is to me."

RUSSELL: "Have you ever known a case where the—or heard of it in any of your study—of anybody that pretended to know anything about it that ever assumed that the heart had anything to do with the emotion?"

WITNESS: "No, sir."

RUSSELL: "Except in theological and religious circles, we use that as a symbol. That isn't the word I am thinking of, but you know what I mean."

WITNESS: "I think it was at one time the theory, until the life of Doctor Harvey when they advanced the idea—"

RUSSELL: (interrupting) "In other words, a born idiot has just as much physical heart as anybody but has no emotion or control over anything."

WITNESS: "Yes."

RE-CROSS EXAMINATION BY MR. RICHARDS

RICHARDS: "Do you think a man could fall in love with a woman, without a heart?"

(Laughter)

RICHARDS: "I would like to have you answer that."

WITNESS: "You mean a physical heart?"

RICHARDS: "Without the ordinary emotions of the heart."

WITNESS: "I will say I don't think there are any emotions of the heart."

RICHARDS: "Well you think that so far as the heart is concerned, a man could have a woman just as well as without it."

WITNESS: "Yes, sir, so far as the heart is concerned."

RICHARDS: "That is all."

WITNESS EXCUSED

This witness, the local school superintendent, who had started testifying about Hassell bringing back his step-children's textbooks suddenly became an expert on criminal psychology and engaged in a pinball exchange of opinions getting at whether Hassell was sane or insane.

And to defense attorney Russell's credit, he led his witness through a landmine without blowing up his client's case. Russell seems to have heard about the witness and jumped at a chance to use him as his main witness without really knowing what he could offer as testimony. That usually spells disaster for a defense attorney, but Russell and Richards seemed to reach an impasse on why Hassell oddly seemed to show few outward signs of emotion despite having slaughtered his family.

Moreover, the witness raised more questions about Hassell with his testimony that the defendant had some unusual religious beliefs, although he seemed quite intelligent about discussing them in a coherent fashion.

Everybody in the courtroom, and particularly those seated in the jury box, were left wondering what Hassell believed in. Did he believe in God? Some other spiritual being? Or maybe nothing? Obviously whatever it was that Hassell talked about during the five-hour jailhouse interview was strange enough that the attorneys and judge determined revealing it would be prejudicial.

With the trial winding down, both the defense and prosecution seemed concerned about answering the obvious question: why would a man kill his family and not flee Parmer County as soon as he could?

Unfortunately that question was not answered in court.

Russell chose to follow his main defense witness with more witnesses who saw Hassell after the murders and observed his demeanor. And there seemed to be some question over when the family was murdered.

Mrs. Lindop, the wife of a prosecution witness and whose first name was not given to the court reporter, was called to the stand.

WITNESS: "I saw the Hassell children on Saturday afternoon, the 4th, out there on the place, the 4th of December."

CROSS-EXAMINATION BY MR. RICHARDS

WITNESS: "My oldest boy also saw them. I don't know whether he is in town now or not . . .

"I saw Mrs. Hassell come out of the door and two of the children. I mean the door of their house, while I was passing in the car on the public road about four or five hundred yards away.

"Between the road and the house, there is a lot of fences and feed piled up, and there is also a barn between there. It is along a big hill-side, too. But I saw her and recognized it to be Mrs. Hassell. It was a pretty afternoon, warm and nice; it was a pretty day. That was the afternoon of the 4th. My son was with me. And there was a boy that I took to be Aldon, unharnessing a team of mules at the barn. Yes, sir, I think I saw Aldon Hassell on the 4th of December. I am certain that was Mrs. Hassell, but I am not so certain that the man was Aldon because they said he was away at the time. Then I saw two smaller children at the door playing at the back door.

"Yes, sir, I am certain that was on the 4th, and I could not be mistaken. That was on the 4th day of December."

WITNESS EXCUSED

V. Tate was then called to the stand by counsel Russell.

"I conducted the Hassell farm sale out at the Hassell place on the 22nd of December and had occasion to observe the defendant, George J. Hassell."

RUSSELL: "Did you see anything unusual or out of the ordinary about his demeanor or conduct as far as you could tell? He acted perfectly normal, did he? He didn't act like a man that killed nine people and had them buried there on the premises walking over their graves all the time, did he?"

WITNESS: "I don't know as I could say about that."

RICHARDS: "We object to that."

RUSSELL: "Take the witness."

RICHARDS: "No questions."

RUSSELL: "Stand aside."

WITNESS EXCUSED

Jurors would get a bit more information about Hassell from the next witness.

"My name is Claude Benton, and I am Sheriff of Deaf Smith County, Texas.

"I had occasion on Friday evening of last week to conduct this defendant to the Hereford jail from Farwell. Another officer was with me. Mr. Hassell talked freely and laughed and joked with us. He also talked freely about the crimes he had committed and went into detail as to this alleged crime for which he is on trial. He didn't seem to be worried about the matter in the least.

"He said he had on the next-to-the-oldest boy's shoes—the boy that he had killed. And he apparently thought that was perfectly all right. And he said 'Well about all the clothes—' no, he said he had on none of his own clothes, except his underwear. He said the suit belonged to his dead brother.

"Over Saturday and Sunday, I had occasion to bring him his meals and observed that he was always cheerful. Every time I saw and talked with him, he appeared to be in a cheerful mood.

"His wounds were dressed in the Hereford jail last Sunday about seven or eight o'clock, and I noticed him joking with the doctor.

RUSSELL: "I don't know what I am going to get when I ask you this question: Did he make any statement to you or in your presence about why he made this confession? It was offered in evidence here."

RICHARDS: "We object to that, your honor, as being immaterial and irrelevant."

JUDGE: "Sustain that objection."

RUSSELL: "Take the witness."

CROSS-EXAMINATION BY MR. RICHARDS

"I said he did tell us about quite a number of crimes, and he told us the nature of them. He told us about committing a crime in California and didn't tell us the name of the town. He told us about several different places; none of them were serious crimes though. He told us about joining the Army, and what he did in the army, and how long he served.

"I really don't know whether he told us about his marriage to Minnie Laughlin (sic) or not, but he said he had married three times.

"He told us about framing up on a man in Arizona or New Mexico, and it seemed to me like that was more or less serious.

"He told us he joined the navy and about serving a term in the penitentiary at Leavenworth. It was a good long story he told us. And he told us about the offense about which he is now charged; he told just about a period of his life covering about twenty years.

"Yes, sir, he told us how many days intervened between the killing of eight members of his family and the killing of Aldon Hassell."

(Objection sustained on how many days)

RE-DIRECT EXAMINATION BY MR. RUSSELL

"Mr. Hassell said he got away only with a part of that scheme they framed up on a man in Arizona.

"He laughed and talked about all of these things apparently as if the whole thing was a joke and talked just as unconcerned about this affair as you and I would talk about going duck hunting. He showed absolutely no emotion of any description."

WITNESS EXCUSED

MR. RUSSELL: "The defendant rests."

REBUTTAL WITNESS BY MR. RICHARDS

"My name is R. E. Maddex, and I live one block west of the Court House in Parmer County, Farwell, Texas. We do a retail hardware business in Texico, New Mexico.

"I know the defendant. He had some business dealings with me throughout the year of 1926, considerable business for a farmer. We had some business transactions with him along in December 1926. We had sold him some implements and signed some notes in favor of a company in Dallas. When the notes came due, he couldn't pay them this year, and he came in there and extended them on until next year with additional security; and that is the transaction he was in there for. That was along about the fifth or sixth of December. Then he was in there again about the 15th or 16th of December, after he decided to sell out to Mr. Lindop, and he came in our place of business to get his security released and the debt transferred. He seemed a little nervous at that time."

WITNESS EXCUSED

Plaintiff Closed.

Defendant Closed.

The transcript does not state what time the session concluded and when the jury began deliberations. It did not take long, however.

The Verdict

Sedalia Democrat, Sedalia, Missouri, January 14th, 1927:

> Jury delivered verdict of guilty of a single count of murdering Aldon, twenty-one, after two-day trial in district court. The death penalty was recommended. Jury deliberated less than two hours.
>
> Hassell sat unmoved as the verdict was read shortly before one o'clock this morning, and when led to his cell, maintained the same indifference shown since his arrest recently when the bodies of his wife and her children were found in a dug out on their ranch near here.
>
> The trial required only two days and consisted mostly of reading of Hassell's confession. No announcement was made as to the disposition of the remaining eight indictments against him charging murder.

One remarkable fact about the proceedings is the speed with which Hassell was tried and convicted and the subsequent appeal by his attorney, who argued to Judge Tatum that the jury was tainted by pre-trial publicity.

Although not clear from news stories or the trial transcript, Hassell probably was moved immediately from the town of Farwell, either to a nearby town's jail or to the state prison in Huntsville to await his execution by the electric chair.

Questions Linger

So many questions pop up when reading the Hassell trial transcript. What was the prosecution's strategy at trial? Why didn't jurors hear more about the killings—for instance an autopsy report to verify Hassell's version of the murders? Was Hassell really getting ready to flee Farwell? Why did he have to kill a baby and other small children if his intent was simply to cover up Maudie's pregnancy; why not just kill Maudie and Susan? Why didn't he just leave town instead of killing his family?

Did Sheriff Martin conduct a full interrogation of Hassell in addition to the confession? Such an interrogation could have lasted hours if Sheriff Martin had gone through the timeline of the Hassells from the point of the couple's marital problems to the point where he attempted suicide.

Answers are mostly impossible to find because so little was written—either in court briefs or news accounts—following the conviction.

Why didn't the prosecutor spend more time questioning the surviving daughter Nora, Susan's father, and Susan's brother? It seems the testimony from members of the Ferguson family served only to show jurors how much Hassell had emotionally devastated them.

Another question: what kind of religious oddball was Hassell? Why even question the Farwell schools' superintendent about this religious angle without giving jurors more details?

What was all that vague testimony about Hassell's unusual view on religion? What had Hassell told police regarding his life story that was too prejudicial to divulge at trial? Did the superintendent ever publish any analysis of Hassell?

If jurors were interested, they might have cornered the prosecutor or defense attorney outside the courtroom to find out more details about the murders and what these attorneys really thought happened. Judges today invite jurors to wait and talk to attorneys after the trial is concluded, so attorneys can get an idea of how well they handled their case. Jurors can be brutally honest and often have lots of questions about points of evidence that seemed intentionally brief or even unclear.

Prosecutor Richards pounded each witness who had contact with Hassell about the defendant's demeanor before or after the murders. Was Hassell nervous? Did he show any emotion or remorse? Although we don't have any news accounts or closing arguments to study, Richards' case sought to prove that Hassell knew what he was doing and was sane.

Defense attorney Russell, strapped for time to build a decent defense for his client, cross-examined each prosecution witness, seeking to paint a picture of a man so calm and cold that he must have been insane to have committed such an atrocity.

George Hassell's confession provides a motive for his rampage. He killed to cover up the unforgivable act of raping his young niece and getting her pregnant. Once he had killed Aunt Susan, he couldn't (or did not want to) stop the slaughter.

That, according to today's generation of psychologists, is typical of what is now known as a family annihilator. Simply put these killers—mostly white men in their thirties—wipe out their families for complex reasons, such as money problems or some other threatening family issue.

Robert DeLong, another psychologist friend now retired in New Zealand, read the trial transcript and thought Hassell's actions could be that of a psychopath.

Dr. Tammy McCoy-Arballo, a former news colleague who now is a clinical psychologist in Southern California, reminded me that ethics prohibit psychologists or psychiatrists from diagnosing somebody they have not personally interviewed or diagnosed.

So is there anything we can we assume about Hassell's mental state?

McCoy-Arballo, without specifically diagnosing Hassell, points to a potential answer: antisocial personality disorder as defined by the American Psychiatric Association and their *Diagnostic and Statistical Manual of Mental Disorders*. This is the association's description of the disorder:

> Antisocial personality disorder describes an impairment pattern of behavior in which individuals consistently disregard and violate the rights of others around them.
>
> The disorder is best understood within the context of the broader category of personality disorders. A personality disorder is an enduring pattern of personal experience and behavior that deviates noticeably from the expectations of the individual's culture, is pervasive and inflexible, has an onset in adolescence or early adulthood, is stable over time, and leads to personal distress or impairment.

> The symptoms of antisocial personality disorder can vary in severity. The more egregious, harmful, or dangerous behavior patterns are referred to as sociopathic or psychopathic. There has been much debate as to the distinction between the two descriptions. Sociopathy is chiefly characterized as something severely wrong with one's conscience; psychopathy is characterized as a complete lack of conscience regarding others. Consequences of this disorder can include imprisonment, drug abuse, and alcoholism.
>
> People with this illness may seem charming on the surface, but they are likely to be irritable and aggressive, as well as irresponsible. They may have numerous somatic complaints and perhaps attempt suicide. Due to their manipulative tendencies, it is difficult to tell whether they are lying or telling the truth.

The bad news for those with this disorder: "There is no clearly indicated treatment for antisocial personal disorder," according to the *DSM*.

Hassell admitted that he had a violent streak dating back to when his dad died, and he suspected his step-mother of poisoning his father. He wanted to kill the "whole bunch" (family) but instead got drunk on whiskey, he confessed.

Even though more than ninety years has passed since Hassell's execution, he leaves enough descriptions of his personality to suggest that he fits the pattern of a psychopath. He seemed to kill without conscience and yet appeared to most as one of the most likable people any neighbor might want. "What a nice guy," everybody said, and all the kids seemed to like him so much, and he was always so helpful. Those neighbors might have told a journalist who knocked on the door after Hassell's vicious crime was discovered that there was no outward sign he could be that violent. Somebody like Hassell can hide in plain sight until something triggers him to commit violence.

Unlike Sheriff Martin and his deputies in the tiny Parmer County community, today's law enforcement community is well-equipped and trained, as well as connected to all the necessary experts who use sophisticated tools to solve crimes and apprehend the bad guys.

The local prosecutor relied on the physician who treated Hassell's self-inflicted wounds to double up as a mental health expert and determine if the defendant was sane and could stand trial.

Today law enforcement can tap the nation's scientists and mental health specialists to understand why and how a crime was committed, plus determine if there are behavior patterns that could help track down the culprit or link him to other similar crimes.

The Federal Bureau of Investigation, with its army of technicians working from sophisticated laboratories, and U.S. Marshal Service with its long and celebrated history of hunting down fugitives, both have Behavior Analysis Units that can provide local, state, and federal law enforcement officials with insights into the minds of criminals.

My step-son, Craig, a former U.S. Marine Corps military policeman and a chief inspector of U.S. Marshal Service who has a distinguished career in tracking and capturing fugitives, helped me get in touch with an expert he has consulted on cases.

At the Marshal's BAU in Washington, D.C., its chief is psychologist Dr. Melanie Malterer, whose expertise is often sought by USMS investigators like Craig at crime scenes nationwide. Previously at U.S. Bureau of Prisons for thirteen years, Dr. Malterer has been at USMS since 2015.

Family annihilators are a relatively rare type of killer, she said. Only a handful or more are reported annually. One who murders two different families is even more rare, she added. Americans with their access to firearms seem to outnumber other nationalities for cases of family annihilators, the psychologist said. Mostly male, family annihilators are typically white and in their thirties, and who experience some personal event that triggers such a violent outburst.

The earliest recorded U.S. case Dr. Malterer has read about was the January 19th, 1900 case of major league baseball player Martin Bergen, who murdered his wife and two young children in their North Brookfield, Massachusetts home, then committed suicide. As with Hassell's crime, the murders by the twenty-nine-year-old catcher for the Boston Beaneaters were a widely reported crime.

A more recent case, she said, that garnered widespread press attention was the August 13th, 2018 murder of thirty-four-year-old Shannan Watts, pregnant with a son, and two daughters, four-year-old Bella and three-year-old Celeste, who initially were reported missing by Shannan's husband, Chris Watts, thirty-three, an oil worker from Frederick, Colorado, north of Denver.

Chris Watts was dealing with some serious personal problems, investigators found. The couple previously filed for bankruptcy, and Chris Watts began a relationship with another woman who thought Watts had left his family. Usually family annihilators commit suicide to avoid the public humiliation of his actions. But Watts denied any involvement in his family's death, only later confessing to strangling his wife and smothering his young daughters and telling authorities where he hid the bodies.

A common profile of family annihilators, Dr. Malterer says, is somebody becoming so desperate about his situation that he chooses to eliminate his wife and children to spare them the embarrassment or indignity of his actions.

That would describe Hassell's predicament of seeing his stepdaughter's pregnancy becoming more apparent and the scandal he surely faced when his sexual assault of a fourteen-year-old became public knowledge. He confessed as much to Sheriff Martin and the county attorney.

In studying Hassell's crimes, I keep reminding myself this occurred during a time when criminology wasn't the science it is today, and the care of mentally ill or troubled individuals was still quite primitive. Hassell's prime defense witness is an enlightening example demonstrating how little was known about such troubles at the time.

The one common thread about killers I have seen from my experience interviewing them and attending their court cases is that killers often look quite "normal," and they usually don't act strangely. It is only when witnesses describe the heinous actions of the defendant that they provide a glimpse beyond the mask of a psychopath. And in court, that mask still protects the killer from any outward reaction. They usually don't show shame, shock, or remorse.

Ted Bundy of Tacoma, Washington, a handsome law school student, persuaded pretty college coeds to accompany him by using his charm to catch them off guard. He then brutally raped and murdered perhaps as many as fifty women. Journalists interviewed people who knew Bundy; they voiced shock to think he could commit the crimes of which he was accused. I went to church with Bundy's mom, a most sweet and proud lady. Only when he escaped from a Colorado courtroom and then committed the vicious murders in Florida at a sorority house did the most sinister side of the man, who always professed innocence, become so shockingly apparent. Working on that story while a journalist in Washington, I just could not fathom the depravity of Bundy, who had been so manipulative and convincing in his pleas of innocence.

Killers are mentally sick, but to what extent are they too insane to be tried for their crimes? The usual insanity standard questions whether a defendant knew right from wrong during the commission of his crime. Russell did his best to persuade jurors to question Hassell's mental condition via a witness, the school superintendent, who said he was a graduate student of sociology and criminology. The witness, however, did not seem to want to interview Hassell about his specific crimes. He seemed more fascinated by Hassell's unorthodox religious beliefs than the fact that the defendant had killed two separate families.

Following the trial, defense attorney Russell quickly filed his appeal of the conviction. Russell writes that Judge Tatum ruled on December 29th to convene a special session on Monday, January 3rd, to select a grand jury. The jury deliberated on the case the next day and returned an indictment of capital murder, indicting Hassell for the murder of his step-son Aldon. On January 5th, the sheriff was ordered to summon jurors on January 7th. Also, that day Hassell was brought to court and Judge Tatum appointed Judge Russell to represent the defendant.

Russell was concerned about the speed with which the case was proceeding and filed a motion to move the trial out of Farwell, where tempers were at a flash point. The judge immediately overruled the motion. Hassell refused to enter a plea, and Judge Tatum set the trial to begin. The two-day trial ended January 12th with a guilty verdict and recommendation that the judge condemn Hassell to death. Russell said he moved for a new trial, which Judge Tatum immediately denied.

Judge Tatum had sentenced Hassell to die before he could reasonably mount a case for a new trial, Russell complained to the court. Russell pleaded that the Texas rule for change of venue—that a defendant must supply two affidavits from prospective jurors supporting such change—was impossible to satisfy because of the public furor over the murders and the anger directed at the defendant.

"Affiant states that he has talked with a number of influential citizens of said Parmer County, some of whom admitted to affiant that there was a dangerous prejudice against said defendant, but such citizens failed and refused to sign said supporting affidavit.

"Affiant further says that there is a dangerous feeling among the citizens of this county against the defendant, and this affiant has been informed by credible citizens of this county that people, meaning some of the people of the county and others who may attend this trial, that they were merely waiting to ascertain the verdict of this court and jury in this case, and if the said verdict was not to their satisfaction that they, meaning said people, would attend to the defendant themselves, meaning that there would be an attempt to 'mob' or take the life of the defendant in the case said verdict was not to the satisfaction of them."

Russell said it was a "farce" to attempt a fair and impartial trial and that the atmosphere was so hostile that jurors were afraid to render any other verdict than a death sentence.

The appeal for a new trial and change of venue presented to Judge Tatum barely landed on the bench before the judge dismissed it, Russell said. The attorney said he did not have time to investigate and procure witnesses to establish a defense that Hassell had not been responsible for his actions because of temporary insanity.

In a surprising dig at the judge, Russell said Hassell was tried by prospective jurors who already had made up their minds and condemned him before they were selected as jurors and that they heard a case presided over by a "judge whose ear appeared to be on the ground listening to the voice of the people."

Russell no doubt had appeared before Tatum on other cases and very well may have been a fellow judge in the same judicial district. In a small town in a sparsely populated county, Russell had taken a swing at a judge who appeared to enjoy the support of most citizens. If the case earned Tatum a lot of favorable press and support; Russell, on the other hand, may have torched his career. A search of news stories shows only one story in the following years after the trial involving Russell: a probate matter.

Meanwhile more stories were appearing every week following the trial. Hassell just kept on talking to jailers in the weeks following his conviction. On February 1st, 1927, the *Austin American-Statesman* had the following to say in reference to Hassell's first family of victims in Whittier, California.

Police Digging for Hassell's Victims

> "Hassell, according to a letter received from Sheriff L.L. Leward of Walker County, Texas, confessed recently that ten years ago he killed a woman with whom he was living here [in Whittier] and her three adopted children, burying their bodies beneath the house.
>
> "Guided by a chart prepared by Hassell, police in relays last night had dug their way through hard clay to a point which they estimated to be within two feet of where the bodies should be found. When the digging was concluded for the night, a pit five feet deep and five feet long had been made. Because of the cramped quarters, only one man was permitted to dig at a time."

The same newspaper then reported on February 16th about an appeal in progress and then a request by Hassell's family to delay the imminent execution until all avenues were exhausted, to protect Hassell's rights.

"Appeal of George J. Hassell will be made to the court of criminal appeals in Austin seeking to avoid death in the electric chair Feb. 25, to which he has been sentenced. Governor Dan Moody has declined to commute the sentence to imprisonment but said he will grant a stay of execution if necessary to enable the courts to pass on Hassell's sanity.

Hassell is now on death row in Huntsville, awaiting execution."

The appeal was still in progress when the *Gazette* in Montreal, Quebec reported this on March 23rd, 1927:

"AUSTIN. TEXAS, MARCH 23rd, George J. Hassell of Farwell, Texas, confessed slayer of thirteen persons, sentenced to die March 25th, was today granted a second thirty-day stay of execution by Governor Dan Moody. The stay was granted in order that Hassell might file an appeal. Hassell's family sought and received the stay of execution from the governor to delay the execution."

The Road to Farwell

As I researched my great aunt's murder and studied the trial transcript, I often daydreamed about Farwell. What did it look like in 1926, and what would I find if I were to visit? As I waited for the long train to clear the crossing and reveal my destination, I wondered what the town of Farwell, the focus of my research for so long, would reveal to me. It was a magical moment for me, both as a writer and a family member, to return to the crime scene. I was most interested in learning where the trial had occurred. For some reason, I had conjured an image that the trial was held in some temporary setting in the absence of a bona fide courthouse. I had an image of a small cowboy town that was tough and dealt with bad guys so efficiently that it didn't need a courthouse.

I had hemmed and hawed about visiting Farwell, almost 1,000 miles from my home in Southern California, for five years. My wife, Bev, fed up with my excuses and impatient for me to finish this project, had finally began planning the trip for me to get this important trip under way. If I needed more time, I could come back, I thought.

Highway 84 through New Mexico, another east-west corridor to the south of the busier Highway 40, runs through wild country that William Bonny, a.k.a. Billy the Kid, roamed as a cowboy and outlaw in the 19th century. His gravesite in Fort

Sumner is a wonderful diversion from the empty high plains that occasionally reveals a small rancher making a meager living raising cattle or horses. Mostly the high country looks like a long, tiring journey from one of the Zane Grey novels my mother so loved. Fort Sumner provides an amazing green spot because of the Pecos River flowing southward. Other than the Pecos, the terrain shows nothing but scrub and an occasional tree on land so dry, it made me instinctively lick my lips.

Why did George and Susie Hassell pick Farwell to settle, such a long distance from Blair, Oklahoma, where the Ferguson clan had settled in the southwest corner of the state? I had this and many other questions, and Texas author Lana Payne Barnett, whose book about a trilogy of murders in the Texas Panhandle which included the Hassell massacre, offered to introduce me to some people who could help. She scheduled our meeting at Godfather's Pizza. I offered to buy the pizzas and any refreshments.

Farwell, just across the Burlington North Santa Fe railroad tracks that separates it from Texico, New Mexico, did not grow in population as civic leaders envisioned when the railroad decided to base regional operations in Clovis. Before and after the railroad operations came Clovis, it probably remained the same size of sixteen hundred or so. Today it is home to about thirteen hundred people.

Dominating the skyline is a huge grain storage facility, and the major business is a tractor dealership that looks to be profitable, as any farm-based business should in this part of the state. Farwell holds a secret that misleads those who whiz by on Highway 84 and barely have time to look left and right before they are on their way out of town. Most of the historic town is nestled around a civic square on the south side of the highway, a half dozen blocks away, where long-haul truckers and that busy railroad make it difficult to slow down and explore the hidden Farwell that is such a jewel.

Several hundred neat brick or stone homes line quiet streets. A beautiful Victorian mansion offers a glimpse of what Farwell's founders built in the past. The local churches are clustered together, each one very apparent that they are well-attended on Sundays and supported by their devout congregations.

I found our meeting place, Godfather's Pizza, without trouble. In fact it's about the sole eatery in Farwell and was filled with people lining up for pizza, salads, or sandwiches, mostly take-out orders. I sat at a table and began watching as I waited while six women celebrated a birthday. They brought their own cake. As people came in to order food, the women seemed to know most everybody in town and joyfully accepted birthday best wishes from friends.

I identified Lana Payne Barnett from her portrait in her book when she walked inside with her daughter, Tamala. It had been an hour or more drive for them from Tulia to the north. Texans are used to driving far distances, she said. A celebrity in her native Panhandle for her books and newspaper articles, Lana is a delightful person still writing history after retiring from newspaper journalism. She introduced me to David Stevens, then editor of the *Clovis Eastern New Mexico News*, and an avid history buff. Next to join us was Will Anderson, a retired Navy commander who teaches politics and government at Clovis Community College. Will is a native son and witness to Farwell's history since his grandparents settled there. Each person had a story to tell me, but they all wanted to learn a bit more about my motives before we got down to business. I could appreciate their hesitancy to open up to a complete stranger about something that rocked their hometown ninety years ago. I showed them an old photograph of Aunt Susie and her sisters, which included my grandmother as a young girl. That seemed to warm them up, and we began eating some delicious pizza. They were anxious to take me to the murder site, the old courthouse, and the historic Mount Olivet Cemetery, where my relatives are buried.

Will, a lanky and youthful sixty-something and grandson of Farwell's sole surviving banking family, invited me to ride with him in his pickup as we first headed eastward on Highway 84 and then turned onto a farm road into a vast green expanse of lush wheat that unfolded as far as I could see. We then turned onto a dirt side road and drove for another mile.

"I used to ride my bicycle out here all the time." He slowed as he hunted for the spot. There was nothing to distinguish the site of the murder from any other patch of grassland along the road until he spotted a road that bisected the main dirt road we were following. There some old wooden sheets of plywood cast aside on the ground drew our interest, but I dismissed any fanciful notions as I realized that anything wooden would have deteriorated over ninety years. The farmhouse was long gone.

Farwell residents Will Anderson and David Stevens at site of Hassell farmhouse

I thought about my great-aunt and her daughter walking into town during those final days to see a doctor about Maudie's pregnancy. I could see the Llano Estacado is so flat that there is nothing to conceal anyone's activity, even at some distance. Still nobody heard screams or gunfire coming from the farmhouse when the murders occurred. Lana, who had been to this site when she was researching her murder trilogy, seemed just as moved by the experience as I was. I tried to envision the Hamlin rental on the flat terrain, not far from a dirt road. It seemed quite a distance to walk into town from the site, but people were used to walking in those days. It was cold that day as Susan and Maudie walked to town. I wondered what they talked about as they trudged along the dirt road, wind whipping the dust around them, or whether they suffered in silence, anticipating unwelcome news from the doctor.

My next thought was that this didn't look like the terrain I had envisioned. Somehow I thought the land would be hilly and that the Hassells had picked a spot with rolling wheat fields unfolding below a house situated on a hill. I wanted to linger, but my new friends wanted to show me more.

Will was late for one of his government classes but wanted to show me the cemetery. Mount Olivet Cemetery, named for the Mount of Olives in old Jerusalem, was on the opposite end of town, about four miles south of Farwell. On one side of the road was New Mexico, and on the other was Texas. The cemetery had been freshly mowed. Only a few trees dotted the property, which once was owned by the huge XIT Ranch. Large livestock feed yards surrounded the cemetery. I found this cemetery extremely compelling. A sign proclaimed the name, and a dirt road snaked through the grounds. The most recent burial was in 1977, I was told. Only about 200 graves have stone markers. Historians know there are far more graves that became hidden or deteriorated over time. They had once enlisted a woman who had a gift for finding stuff in the ground, including water, and had her cover the entire cemetery grounds with her "witching stick," which dipped to the ground each time she discovered a grave. Each of the forgotten graves was marked with a steel rod. The poor souls buried there had their wooden grave markers deteriorate over time. Now history buffs were caring for the cemetery and planning improvements to the grounds as soon as funds could be raised for proper stone markers. Nobody knows the identity of those souls, but they should be remembered, nonetheless.

Dave Kube, then Curry County Fire Marshal, arrived to tell me about the work he and Teresa Ancire, a Parmer County probation officer, had begun to honor those buried at the cemetery, which had been largely ignored and abandoned for so many years. Neither could stand to see a piece of Parmer County history further deteriorate and disappear. They were fascinated by the graves of twelve infants they believe were stillborn children of the Cannon Air Force Base service people. They arranged to have markers created in their honor. They also could not ignore the white stone marker near the cemetery entrance that had barely legible inscriptions.

They pointed out the place where Susan and the children were buried. I saw a marker and slowly walked toward it, emotion building with each step. I touched the marker and traced the letters with my finger. The white marble felt smooth, and I could only discern any inscription as a slight scratch on the surface. I looked closely and could see the name Susan. The rows of names, all nine of them, looked as though each had ages but no dates of birth. It must have been a huge expense for the community to buy this stone at a time when most were buried with simple wooden crosses. I felt tears welling in my eyes for family I barely knew until five years ago but now felt such an emotional connection with.

Author at Hassell family gravestone paid for by Farwell citizens

Teresa Ancira respectfully approached me after a few moments.

'"With your permission, we'd like to put some stone down around the grave, maybe a little fence."

I told her that was a wonderful idea, and I fought back tears again. Teresa said she and Dave had been able to make improvements at the cemetery with donated labor and funds.

Newspaper editor David wondered whether the Hassell children were buried around their mother or lined up side-by-side. He had read articles that included both descriptions. All able-bodied men in the area had come to help dig this mass grave. Many toiled, I'm sure, with growing anger over the killer being held in a jail just a few miles away.

I would go back to the grave later to reflect on the scene and the victims.

Will, whose college students were patiently waiting for him, wanted to take me to the courthouse before he had to return to teach.

A handsome Texan complete with hat and boots, Will told me that he and his childhood buddies used to ride their bicycles to the cemetery on Halloween "to see if we could find any ghosts." As we approached the courthouse, he pointed out the old two-story stone jail that has been gutted of all iron bars and remains only as an historic monument. Built in 1917, the jail stands without a plaque, however.

When Hassell was confined in the jail, the structure was only one story. Will said kids used to come up to the open-air window and talk to Hassell, who peered out from the bars. In later years, Will said he used to do the same thing with prisoners waiting for trial or serving their sentences. In Farwell, where the winters are very cold and the summers are blistering, the old jail relied on a Texas breeze to ventilate the stuffy confines via open windows.

As we walked past the jail, I was introduced to the county sheriff.

Parmer County Sheriff Randy Geries, a lawman who looked as though he didn't really need any deputies to help him keep the peace, showed me a picture of his predecessor, Sheriff James Martin, who served from 1923 until 1930. Although all the sheriff's records prior to 1946 have disappeared, Geries said he believes Martin was so concerned about the possibility of a lynching of Hassell by an angry mob breaking into the jail that he asked the county commissioners to build a new jail after the Hassell trial concluded.

Geries has framed and placed a picture near his office of the blueprint for a proposed two-story jail that included upstairs quarters for the sheriff and his family, who were expected to care for the prisoners and launder their clothes, plus segregated cells for whites on one side and blacks on the other on the first floor. The jail was never built, but Geries' department eventually got a modern jail that connects with its modern headquarters and vehicle maintenance section.

Geries said he has no idea whether Martin left law enforcement or remained in the area. "All those records are gone." He sounded frustrated.

We continued walking.

The old three-story courthouse is probably the tallest building for miles around, except for the grain elevator off the main highway. It is not far from the sheriff's headquarters and is near the center of the 586 original acres surveyed for Farwell and granted to the county by Capitol Freehold Land Investment

Company, London, England. A spacious lawn, adjacent to a veterans park commemorating all the Farwell lives lost during America's wars and conflicts, now surrounds it. When I visited, the main entrance to the building had been closed because of seismic upgrades and installation of an elevator. When first planned, the county budgeted no more than $50,000 in 1913, and officials moved into their new quarters in 1917.

We were on our honor to enter this courthouse without any weapons. There was no screening. Will left his handgun in the pickup and told me not to worry about my pocketknife as we entered a building that had no uniformed officers at its entrance. In fact we looked to be the only visitors.

We rode the elevator to the second-floor courtroom. There used to be a loft for overflow seating. That has now been paneled over and converted to office space. The courtroom is no different than any other courtroom. It looked as though it could seat several hundred in blonde wooden former pews donated by the First Baptist Church. Lana, her daughter Tamala, and I sat there and talked about the emotions of the trial that day, not long after New Year's, 1927.

I had read that my great-grandfather had been seated with Susie's brothers, maybe a sister, and her daughter Nora. They probably took their places behind the prosecutors, which is the traditional seating arrangement for victims in criminal trials. The jury box is also closest to the prosecutor, and he no doubt wanted jurors to see every trace of anguish on the faces of the Ferguson family.

Courthouse relatively unchanged from time of infamous trial

Sitting in the empty courtroom, I imagined the room filling with Farwell's outraged citizens coming to hear what one of their neighbors had done to his family. The emotion I felt at the cemetery was strangely absent. I could only chalk that up to my excitement at finally seeing the very spot where Hassell was convicted. Mostly I was impressed that Farwell had such a grand courthouse back then. The hometown of my youth, twice the size of Farwell, had a small police station but not much more.

As I sat in the handsome pews, Deputy Clerk Rose Longley brought me all the files they had regarding the trial. All that remained were the indictments. Each of the nine file folders contained a charge of murder against Hassell.

Regardless of cost, I asked that she make me a copy of the indictment for the murder of Aunt Susie for my files. Then I casually told her that I had the trial transcript. She seemed excited by that revelation.

Rose told me that many years ago a clerk had given the trial transcript to somebody, and they had never returned it, despite that being nearly as serious an offense as first-degree theft. I immediately decided I wanted them to have the complete historical record. I gave Rose my copy to duplicate for their files.

I stayed with the clerks and chatted about the history of Parmer County. Teresa and her colleagues treated me as royalty and wanted to hear what I had researched on the case. She brought me a book to help me better understand the county's history. I did not realize until later how important this book, *A History of Parmer County, Texas,* by the Parmer County Historical Society, would be to my research.

Before Will dashed off to teach his class, he told me he had an idea what had brought the Hassells to Farwell. Although they leased the farmhouse and land from the most important man in town, they may have had an arrangement to buy the land once they brought in their crop, he said.

That made perfect sense, and the more I read about Farwell's early history, the more I believed that could have been the incentive that led to George and Susie Hassell picking up stakes and moving to a completely new home.

George Hassel threw away his chance for a meaningful life in this friendly town that had offered him a future.

The Birth of Farwell

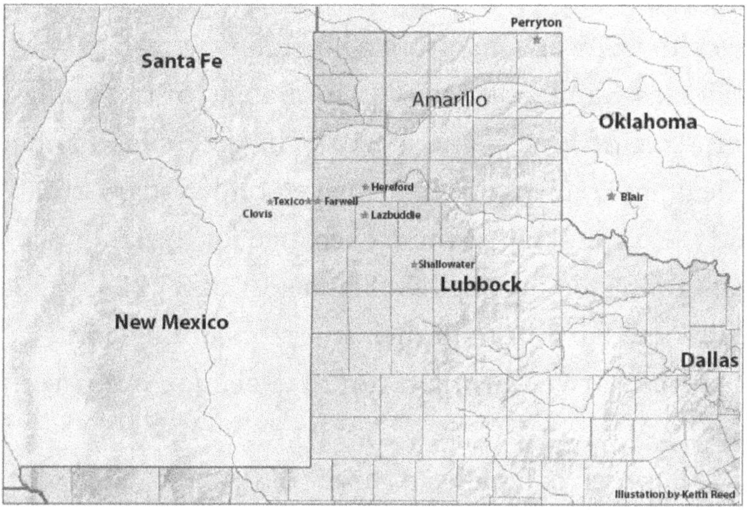

Farwell, not Fairwell or Farewell. The name intrigued me when I first read it and had trouble locating it on a map. Every town's name conveys a point in history when people decided to honor somebody or something. For such a small town today, Farwell provided some important historical characters that made a lasting contribution to the Texas Panhandle. And one of them, it turns out, probably inspired George Hassell to take up residency in Farwell.

When Texas Tech's library sent me a copy of the several pages containing a description of that Christmas holiday time when Hassell became infamous, I wondered about the origin of the research. Turns out the pages came from a book, published in 1974 by the Parmer County Historical Society, that contains a Master of Arts thesis by Eugene V. Sofford, providing a detailed look at a fifty-year period of Farwell beginning in 1905. I got the book in Farwell during my visit, thanks to members of the small but energetic historical society.

The town's namesakes, brothers Charles and John Farwell, were wealthy Chicago investors who became interested in building the Texas Capitol structure in exchange for obtaining three million acres of high plains country in the Texas Panhandle. Their dealings resulted in a law enacted on February 20th, 1879, to build the Capitol in Austin in exchange for the land. The Capitol was completed in April 1888 at a cost of $3,224,593.45, financed by the Farwells and their investors in England.

What the Farwell brothers got in exchange was a veritable treasure.

A. C. Babcock completed a survey of the new ranch that covered 950 square miles on April 27th, 1882.The partnership then created the XIT Ranch, which would operate and compete with a number of other giant ranches in Texas. My guide, Will Anderson, Farwell native, said the letters XIT made it very difficult for rustlers, who regularly raided the plains for livestock, to rebrand with their own bogus brands. The ranch became a formidable kingdom as John Farwell went to Europe to line up funds to purchase livestock and necessary capital to run such a huge empire. The Capitol Freehold Land and Investment Co., Ltd., was formed with $15 million in invested funds.

The ranch operated successfully with Hereford, Shorthorn, and Aberdeen-Angus breeds numbering between 125,000 to 150,000 head of cattle. The ranch spread 100 miles from east to west and 200 miles from north to south. However, while the huge spread prospered at first, it then suffered at the hands of outlaw rustlers and the weather. In the winter of 1884, the XIT lost nearly one million acres of grassland to wildfire. Who knows how much livestock and wildlife perished in the inferno?

The huge ranching operation began to liquidate its holdings in the early 1900s after the Santa Fe Railroad laid track from Roswell, N.M. to the little settlement of Texico. James D. Hamlin of Amarillo, who was selling tracts of land in Texico, was hired to be the ranch representative in 1905 and settled in the new community of Farwell, which he was instrumental in helping to develop on donated XIT land. Some 200,000 acres of XIT land comprising Parmer County would be sold, some for as little as $2 an acre. Acres of land were sold with a 10 percent cash payment, and the balance over a nine-year period at six percent interest, the county history recounted.

Hamlin presided over an enormous ranching operation that was slowly shrinking through sales of properties to other ranchers and much smaller operators. Hundreds of cowboys, who basically lived off the land, would eventually come to Farwell to take care of their personal business, do their laundry, and to vote when elections occurred.

Farwell was in need of new people to build what Hamlin envisioned as a prosperous Panhandle community that could compete with Texico and maybe even Clovis. Two of the first Farwell homes were built in 1906, followed by an official U.S. Post Office. Several Texico business owners were convinced to open new businesses in Farwell. Parmer County was formally organized in 1908. Farwell was growing as the railroad brought in new settlers. But the railroad turned on Farwell and Texico when it wanted more land to headquarter its operations than the mere half section of land offered by Farwell's civic leaders. Santa Fe Railroad, to add insult, built a depot on the Texico side of the border.

Still, enterprising businessmen began to open new businesses across from the courthouse, including an entire block built by Judge Hamlin. Just as Farwell was beginning to flourish, an arsonist struck in 1913 setting a fire in a dry goods store that spread to Hamlin's block of buildings. The devastation was so severe that some wondered if Farwell could ever recover.

By the 1920s, businesses were slowly coming to Farwell to provide services for the ranchers. In 1924, the time the Hassells arrived, the Capitol Company was offering to sell some 500,000 acres and was circulating pamphlets offering land perfect for farms. Capitol was very generous with tenant farmers and had a reputation for never foreclosing on loans. According to the history book, the company even loaned money for improvements, such as shrubs and trees.

Water could be found by digging wells 50 to 225 feet deep, and the annual rainfall of 22.8 inches was sufficient for most dry-land farmers who planted milo maize, hay, and sorghum cane.

What could be better for a big family of Hassells than starting a new farm in Farwell? Hassell leased his land and the farmhouse from the Hamlins and then began his fledging enterprise as a farmer.

For a brief moment in Texas Panhandle history, the most heinous killer crossed path with the Farwell's most historic figure and his wife. Although Hassell met The Judge, there seems no record of Judge Hamlin discussing the case of his infamous tenant. But his wife most certainly knew Hassell and his family because she was the landlord who leased the land and farmhouse to the Hassell family and testified at his trial. And Judge Hamlin, according to reports, would have sold the acreage to Hassell with only a modest down payment, had Hassell wanted to buy the land he farmed.

Teresa Ancira, Parmer County's probation officer, thought I could appreciate Farwell and Parmer County far more by reading a book, "The Flamboyant Judge," that recounts the life and experiences of Farwell's famous Judge Hamlin. Published in 1972 long after his death in 1950, the book includes Hamlin's oral history as told to the co-authors, J. Evetts Haley and William Curry Holden. Teresa found a copy of the out-of-print book and sent it to me following my trip to Texas.

A colorful man who made it his business to know any and everybody, Judge Hamlin recounted his encounters with scoundrels and politicians, cattle thieves and killers, friends and enemies, but not one word about the single most tragic incident in Farwell's history. He seemed like a man who would pass the hat for the funeral and burial and donate to purchase the white stone grave marker.

An intellectual who enjoyed drinking whiskey with the cowboys at area saloons, Hamlin was smart enough to avoid giving George Hassell any more attention than necessary in his own personal story. As a judge and attorney, he probably had met characters as blood-thirsty as Hassell but far more honorable than to kill women and children as they slept in their own home. The judge seemed like a man who would only mention Hassell's name in a coarse conversation in a saloon over sips of whiskey.

Hamlin was an imposing figure who knew the rich and powerful, yet often could be found in his favorite saloons where he seemed to conduct much of his business. An admitted alcoholic, Hamlin was a Kentuckian who left home at age twenty-six with a friend intending to strike it rich in the gold fields of the Klondike in 1897.

He stopped in Amarillo, a town of 1,800 then, and began teaching Latin and Greek at a small college he helped found, then studied law with the ten practicing attorneys in the region that included the famed Temple Houston, son of Texas lion Sam Houston, before being accepted to the Texas Bar Association. Amarillo then was the end of the trail for long cattle drives by cowboys pushing their herds to market. The town was loud and exciting, and cowboys were happy to spend every dime on women and drink as cattle barons negotiated prices and sent their herds onward to Kansas City in railroad boxcars. The booming Panhandle and the westward migration of settlers kept Hamlin and the other attorneys busy as Santa Fe Railroad laid track further into the frontier.

Hamlin was an astute businessman who invested in projects that he felt would prosper. His hunches were pretty accurate. Still a single man, Hamlin was hired by the Farwell brothers as their representative in business matters. The giant ranch had its own foreman who ran the operation for many years. After moving to Farwell, Hamlin began construction of a large warehouse in the new Farwell community, as well as a two-story office building that served as his offices, close by to a small hotel called the Farwell Inn that he owned. The town was growing, and Hamlin brought his new bride, the former Kate Nichols, to a spacious home he built in 1906 that became a showcase of collectibles and books. The couple would travel throughout the frontier, particularly Santa Fe, collecting Indian artifacts.

I thought about Hassell being invited to dinner by Kate Hamlin fresh from the murders of his family. What did this buffoon who could barely read think of the library of books and collectibles decorating the mansion? And I was impressed with the graciousness of Kate Hamlin for opening her home out of kindness to this pathological killer.

One story recounted in the book gave me a hint at Hamlin's formidable character. Soon after his marriage, he invested $2,000 to $3,000 into a bank and icehouse after introducing the businessman to the wealthy Farwells still operating out of Chicago. Hamlin could see the businessman was sinking into debt, so he sold his small share of the bank and icehouse. The businessman learned of Hamlin's financial move, which he believed sealed his doom, and spied the judge pulling his horse and buggy in front of the bank one day.

The banker, a "small man that I could have whipped him with my left hand," stormed out of the bank and confronted Hamlin, who was tying up his horse. He pointed a small Smith and Wesson revolver and began cursing Hamlin as he threatened to kill him.

"So I folded my arms over my chest and took the cursing without saying a word," Hamlin recalled. "I had tightly folded my arms that if he did kill me, he could not plead in self-defense."

The banker's tirade went on until a bank teller hurried out to the street and ended the confrontation by ushering his enraged boss back to the bank.

Hamlin thought about revenge. “So I decided that I would shoot him down like a coyote the next time he passed my office,” which was only a block away from the bank. Hamlin went on a two-week bender and forgot about the “small” banker who did lose both the bank and the icehouse.

Hamlin enjoyed a very close personal and professional relationship with the Farwell brothers and their offspring, often traveling to Chicago to visit the company’s five-story wholesale house overlooking the Chicago River.

However, the Farwell brothers entrusted Hamlin to oversee their giant investment in the Panhandle, coming out to visit only “spasmodically,” Hamlin recalled. John Farwell, a devout Christian, did come out to preach to the XIT cowboys in the1890s, passing out religious literature and exhorting them to repent their sins. The cowboys probably felt obligated to give up their sole day off to listen to their boss preach about the after-life.

Farwell has deep roots and had so much promise to families anxious to farm the rich prairie soil. Somehow the town just sputtered as nearby Clovis mushroomed, partly due to the railroad and also because of the military base.

Before I left, I needed to see if my Aunt Susie had been a member of the Hamlin United Methodist Church, which was founded by Judge Hamlin’s father. The pastor’s wife was folding church bulletins when I arrived at the church office and inquired about old church membership rolls. We looked through them but found they did not date back to the 1920s, although the church was founded in 1906.

However, I left feeling that my great aunt had worshipped there in the past. I felt somewhat more comforted as I returned to the cemetery for one last visit.

Don't Mess with Texas

Hang 'em high from the nearest oak tree was one way of dealing with criminals from the earliest times, when Texas was a republic. George Hassell probably knew his days were numbered when he summoned Sheriff Martin to his home. He made frequent statements to news reporters and anybody else willing to listen that he was ready to pay the ultimate price for his crimes. I wondered if Hassell heard any stories from jailers or fellow inmates about the process of zapping a human body with 1,800 volts of electricity?

It may or may not have made Hassell feel any less apprehensive about his fate, but Texas ended hangings as a form of execution in the summer of 1923. In its place, the state acquired "Old Sparky" for $5,000, as an electric chair that would more quickly dispose of the condemned defendants at the state prison in Huntsville in eastern Texas. Lynchings had become a problem for the state, and lawmakers perhaps preferred the optics of a different kind of capital punishment.

The state penitentiary in Huntsville was chosen to house the new nine-cell death row, which already had a list of men awaiting execution.

The three authors who wrote *The Rope, The Chair, and The Needle*, about Texas capital punishment between 1923 and 1990 found that 510 defendants had been sentenced to die in the electric chair during that period, but only 361 actually were executed. The others had their sentences commuted. These researchers found that 71 percent of the condemned inmates had been convicted of murder.

By 1923 the authors found that lynchings in Texas had all but disappeared from local communities. But prior to the Civil War, the eastern side of Texas saw a strong influx of Black slaves forced to work the many plantations and ranches owned by Southerners, particularly those moving from slave states, such as Louisiana and Alabama. With the large population of former slaves and their descendants living in the area following the Civil War, racial discord became intense. As many as 200,000 slaves were on the tax rolls of plantation owners in eastern Texas at the outset of the Civil War, the trio discovered.

Hanging was carried out at the local level by sheriffs and town marshals, and the spectacle never ceased to draw a crowd of onlookers anxious to see the condemned dangle and kick and choke to death—or if he was lucky, the drop through the trap door would snap his neck, killing him instantly.

The authors found that 394 hangings occurred before 1923, and 60 percent of those executed were Black men. Only three women murderers were among the total.

Huntsville's warden, Capt. R. F. Coleman, resigned on January 1st, 1924 rather than carry out his new responsibility as the state's designated executioner. The authors found this quote, which speaks volumes for the many opponents of capital punishment, "A warden can't be a warden and a killer, too. The penitentiary is a place to reform a man, not to kill him."

The warden's replacement was found fairly quickly, and Old Sparky was tested in preparation for the first electrocutions. Within minutes of the law's effective enactment, the state executed the first of five condemned men. All were Black.

The researchers found documents listing all the electrocutions after the first five, and Newt DeSilva, an Anglo convicted murderer from Jefferson County, was fifteenth in line, but his sentence was commuted on March 20th, 1925. Sidney Welk, sixteenth in line and a convicted murderer from Dallas County, was the first white person electrocuted in Texas on April 3rd, 1925.

George Hassell was thirty-seventh on the list. He would have had some time to think about his crimes as his case went through the court system.

George Hassell Awaits His Execution

George was headed for Huntsville, the Texas prison housing death row inmates and the well-used electric chair, when his appellate process began shortly after his conviction. The news that he was a condemned man was printed in newspapers seemingly everywhere. His appeal was based on the extensive news coverage prior to the trial and how it could impact jurors' minds about the defendant.

George's attorney was pursuing the appeal on grounds that the trial should have been moved because of the heavy news coverage. Attorney Russell, according to some reports, had been disgusted by his client and was anxious to head home following the trial. He left too soon, however, and because of his hasty retreat, he caused some appellate issues. However, he obviously was a true professional, and despite his error, fulfilled his oath to defend an unsavory client as best he could.

In thirty-five years of newspaper journalism that included numerous capital murder cases, I only covered one case that successfully involved a change of venue and can recall only one other such case. The one I covered involved a county sheriff who was rounded up in a federal racketeering sting about corruption involving a gang that operated a string of topless dancing nightclubs in western Washington and waged a war of arson on its competitors. I had been reporting these curious arson fires at topless joints and seemed to be the only one interested until I found a state liquor agency investigator who shared his suspicions with me. The case hinted of deep corruption within the county sheriff's department and even some dirty county government officials. The demoralized sheriff's department was under suspicion because its leader allegedly had worked with the gang of thugs and arsonists by turning a blind eye to their illicit deeds. Widespread news coverage made hearing the case in Tacoma or Seattle impossible; a federal judge ruled to move the case to San Francisco where all defendants were later convicted in U.S. District Court.

Judges would rather exhaust an entire jury pool of every able-bodied and qualified person within the county before ruling to move a trial to another location at great expense.

The federal racketeering trial I covered in San Francisco involved one spin-off in county Superior Court where that trial judge spent days finding twelve jurors and a half dozen alternate jurors who vowed they could ignore the recent news coverage of the federal trial.

Defense attorney Russell left the courtroom in disgust after the verdict, leaving Hassell without legal representation when he was sentenced by Judge Tatum—a court violation Governor Moody later ruled was grounds for a stay of execution. Telling me she loved to dig and research, author Lana Payne also identified Hassell's sister, Dora Watson of Fort Worth, as the person who initiated the appeals process with pleas for clemency to the governor.

The Marshall *Messenger*, Marshall, Texas, on March 23rd had a bit more detail.

"Hassell was granted a second thirty-day stay of execution by governor. Execution is now set for April 25th, unless high court action results in a 'reverse.'

"In giving the reason for the conduct of clemency, which was recommended by the Board of Pardons, Moody said the death warrant was illegally executed and granted Hassell thirty more days in which to file an appeal and get it heard."

The Amarillo *Globe-Times* printed an update on Oct. 12, 1927 under the headline:

FARWELL MAN FACES DEATH

"AUSTIN, Oct. 12—Only small hope of further court action remained today to shield George J. Hassell of Farwell, Texas, alleged slayer of thirteen persons, from the electric chair to which he was sentenced.

The court of criminal appeals today denied Hassell's motion for rehearing of its action in affirming the death sentence. Further clemency for him is regarded as unlikely, since he already has obtained reprieves to give the appeals court time to act on the case.

Denying the rehearing motion, the court held that the trial was unprejudiced and that Hassell was not proved insane."

With time running out, Hassell needed to be re-sentenced to death by Judge Tatum in Farwell. The Marshall, Texas *Messenger* reported on January 11th, 1928:

> "Farwell, Texas, Jan. 10—George J. Hassell, confessed slayer of thirteen members of his family whose bodies were found in a dugout on his farm near here a year ago, must die in the electric chair at Huntsville February 10th.
>
> Judge Reese Tatum pronounced sentence in district court here this afternoon on the basis of Hassell's conviction of a murder of his eldest stepson, Alton Hassell, nineteen, who was also his nephew."

The Austin *American* also reported that day on the Farwell court appearance with a bit more detail:

> "When asked if he had anything to say as to why sentence should not be pronounced again him (sic), Hassell merely made a polite request that his watch, ring, and clothes be returned to him. He smiled and thanked the court when sentenced had been pronounced.
>
> "Two Texas rangers were ordered to Farwell, Parmer county Tuesday to aid local officers in preventing any possible outbreak when George J. Hassell's execution date is set in district court there."
>
> Hassell had appealed his conviction some months ago. The sentence of the trial court was recently affirmed by the Court of Criminal Appeals here."

George, having languished in Farwell's small jail while awaiting his court appearance, was whisked back to Huntsville. The Lubbock *Morning Avalanche* reported on January 24th:

SLAYER TELLS OTHERS HE'S 'GLAD TO BE BACK'

> HUNTSVILLE, Jan. 23—George J. Hassell, confessed slayer of thirteen persons, who is to be electrocuted on Feb. 10, was placed in the penitentiary here today.
>
> Hassell, who was in the custody of Sheriff J. H. Martin and deputy P. D. Mersfelder of Parmer County, was in high spirits. He grasped the hands of other condemned men and told them he was glad to back with them."

A number of news stories appeared in the weeks before his execution. The El Paso *Times* reported February 4th that the warden visited Hassell in his cell.

> "Supplementing a confession attributed to him several months ago, Hassell declared that in June 1917, he choked to death his first wife, Marie Vogel, her son, and their two foster children whom they adopted from an orphan asylum in Colorado. The four victims were killed at their Whittier, Cal. home and buried by the slayer after which Hassell disappeared.

As in the case of all his victims, Hassell was unable to give a motive for his crimes. "'Something came over me and I did it,' he said."

Mrs. Vogel was a spiritualist, and one night "she had a vision that a light came from the sky and struck the floor of their house," the slayer related. "She said the light point to buried money." Hassell dug a hole under the house. "The money must have been deeper, for I didn't find it," he added. Two weeks later, he killed the family and buried the victims in the excavation."

The Galveston *Daily News* had more detail:

"George J. Hassell, a chubby, fair-haired, rather pleasant faced man of thirty-eight, accused of thirteen murders, two women and eleven children, who occasionally chuckled over incidents in his career not immediately related to the murders, sat in the death cell and told Warden N. L. Speer he was 'glad they had found out' he was telling the truth about the killing of a woman and three children in Whittier, Ca. more than ten years ago.

"I am pleased," he told the warden, "that they have found the bodies, so they wouldn't think I was lying. I have told the truth," he said reflectively, "about everything that has happened in my whole life."

"He would not discuss how he killed the woman and children. 'He did say, however, the warden said that he had strangled the boy, a baby, with a stocking. Reference to the boy brought tears to Hassell's eyes because, he said, it reminded him of his own little son by his first wife."

This was the first emotion he displayed, the paper reported. Hassell appeared outwardly cheerful. He earlier described how his murder of Susan Hassell involved an argument over a stepson. Hassell had changed his previous statement at the last minute and carefully omitted any reference to sexually assaulting Maudie.

Another story was published February 9th, 1928 by the Austin *American*:

HASSELL SANE AND MUST PAY PENALTY RULES GOV. MOODY

Asylum Superintendents Say Condemned Man Okay Mentall

"Gov. Moody, after hearing reports from two state employed sanity experts, Wednesday declined to intervene between George J. Hassell, Farwell, Texas, and the electric chair in which the confessed slayer of thirteen members of his family apparently must die early Friday.

Dr. W. J. Johnson, superintendent of the state insane hospital at San Antonio, and Dr. C. K. Standefer, head of a similar Austin institution, returned Wednesday from Huntsville where they administered mental tests to Hassell. Both pronounced him possessed of ability to distinguish right from wrong and to comprehend the result of deeds. They found he had "knowledge of the nature, quality, and wrongfulness of his acts and we (the doctors) do not believe these acts were uncontrollable. He has very little education but is with a general intelligence commensurate with his environment. He cannot be definitely declared insane, feeble-minded, or epileptic."

Hassell Takes a Seat in the Chair

The death watch began.

For more than a year following his trial, George Hassell resumed his former nomadic lifestyle, but this time in handcuffs and jail attire—plus an armed escort—while he made a celebrity tour of Panhandle jails, eventually entering the state prison at Huntsville.

As a killer many times over, Hassell became an infamous inmate and was likely a very big deal to fellow killers, who had only managed to notch one or two bodies during their crime sprees. Hassell, of course, admitted to the thirteen family members but failed to mention the 1915 murder of a poker player in Chicago. There could be others, but Hassell wasn't discussing anything the cops hadn't already pinned on him or he had already admitted committing.

In a sick sort of way, Hassell probably saw himself as finally rising from the lowest rung of society to become an infamous celebrity, with every move he made or word he said noted by newspapers nationwide.

His infamy did nothing to spare him from taking a seat in Old Sparky in early February 1928.

Austin American, Feb. 10, 1928

HASSELL GOES TO CHAIR FOR MURDER OF YOUNG STEPSON

Negro Sent to Death Few Minutes After Man Who Killed 13

HUNSTVILLE, Feb. 10 (AP)—George J. Hassell went to his death in the electric chair at the state prison here at 12:29 this morning for one of the thirteen murders he had confessed he had perpetrated in widely separated portions of the country at two intervals almost ten years apart.

Hassell was in the death chair eight minutes. He was given three shocks. After the first, he was motionless, at the second, he slumped slightly, and at the third, no movement of his body was apparent. Dr. E. L. Angler, assistant prison physician, pronounced him dead.

Just as Hassell and his guards reached the chair from the adjoining death cell, he faced about. The warden asked him if he had anything to say. Deathly pale but apparently composed, except for a slight tremor, Hassell faced the audience of about twenty-five newspaper men, officials, and prison guards. "I would like to announce to the world," he said, "that I am prepared to meet my God. I have made my confession to God and man. Man does not understand it all, but God does."

Immediately he took his seat, and after the usual preliminaries, the current was turned on by Warden Speer, who was sheltered from public gaze behind a partition.

None of Hassell's relatives witnessed his execution. His two sisters stayed at their hotel and Sam Hassell, a cousin who came from his home in Crockett, joined the throng as it left the warden's office but left it before it reached the death house."

The San Bernardino, California, *Sun* reported:

"Hassell's death was the first of a double execution. The second man was Robert Lee Benton, alias R. L. Stanley, a Negro who killed a white man."

"Just prior to the execution, music from the prison rang out. It included mostly stirring marches."

Hassell's execution provided the only justice that could be had for the families he had slaughtered. He was reviled, by the Ferguson family he so damaged beyond repair, and by the community of Farwell, whom he forced into an unwanted national spotlight. Subsequent generations, it seems to me, did their best never to utter his name again.

One of Susan's sisters, Maude, spotted a 1976 anniversary series about the murders and was concerned enough to write to the Amarillo newspaper and report that it had erred in its reporting. For some reason, the entries referred to the main victim, Susan, as Maude, and she wanted to correct the record. As any journalist will attest, any error of this significance mars the series, regardless of how well it was done otherwise. But the series did generate some new facts. My great aunt Maude, whom I remember meeting as a child, was gracious about her request for a correction. In fact she added important information to the story by answering questions the series failed to incorporate.

Aunt Maude apparently told either an editor or the series reporter that she remembers George Hassell as a hard-working family man who treated his new family with kindness in the first months of the new marriage.

His demeanor changed, however, as George started to "fly into uncontrollable rages" and work the children too hard, she said. She described George becoming enraged during a family discussion about religion. "Do you really believe that when that child dies," he asked, pointing to one of the boys, "he will go straight to Heaven?" Susan affirmed that that was her belief, Maude said.

"Then maybe we should kill all the children and send them to Heaven right away!" George responded.

Farwell's Unwanted Legacy

Susan and George Hassell were relative newcomers to Farwell when they made national headlines. But Farwell residents embraced the Fergusons in their mourning and buried Susan and her children in a community cemetery, raising funds to erect a stone burial marker.

Authorities pushed for justice and quickly summoned jurors and convened a criminal trial that resulted in George Hassell's conviction.

The murders are a sad part of Farwell's history and will forever remain so.

As I was writing this manuscript, Clovis newspaper editor and now publisher David Stevens told me the Texas Historical Commission placed a beautiful memorial on the Olivet Cemetery grounds that commemorates the unidentified infants and the slain Hassell family buried there and the historical significance of the cemetery. This care and generosity by Farwell's finest and the state makes me even more committed to this story and to the tiny community that is so distant but so very close to me in spirit and emotion. The story of Susan and her children is an important chapter in Farwell's history, and it should be remembered and dedicated to the townsfolk of Farwell.

I worked for years on this history, often thinking about my late mother and how she might react to the new information I uncovered. I fear she would not want to have known the grisly details, preferring to remember what she was told as a ten-year-old. And as much as she loved to hear about my career highlights and brag about my achievements, I expect my book-loving mom would not be able to read more than a few pages into this work before feeling deeply wounded by my account of our early relationship and my callous teenage skepticism. I am, however, comforted in knowing that my mom always loved a good story.

Acknowledgments

"Whatcha working on?"

Almost every day in my newspaper career, I either asked that question of news colleagues or answered a colleague about the story I was either reporting or writing. We are a curious lot, and very little happens in a busy newsroom without one reporter asking another about a news story. There is a wonderful tension in a big, noisy newsroom with hundreds of journalists on the phone or furiously working their story on a computer as the deadline nears. And the competitive nature of journalists keeps us curious, maybe a bit envious, about our colleagues' work. Just an encouraging remark can help a reporter make his deadline. But news buddies can also provide a valuable insight or phone number for a source that helps break the story faster and more completely.

At least that was the way I remember it all during what I viewed as the golden days of newspaper journalism before hedge funds scooped up family-owned newspapers and began trimming news budgets to boost profits. After I retired from newspapers, my former colleagues heard about my efforts to research the murder of my great aunt. I particularly appreciate the constant encouragement of Mike Kataoka and Ray Smith. Dan Bernstein, who just finished a book, *Justice in Plain Sight*, is a gifted writer, reporter, and columnist who helped me organize the first part of my manuscript with a colorful prologue. I am indebted to Courtney Burkholder, a veteran book editor who not only polished my manuscript but suggested important edits that greatly improved the story. Not only did Courtney come up with the wonderful title, she smoothed all the many rough spots of my writing and pushed me to answer questions that give deeper insight to readers.

I also owe a great debt to my dear little sister, Kathy Hammond of Granite Bay, California, who helped me understand our mother and offered her memories of conversations with Mom and our grandmother. Through Kathy I reconnected with a cousin, Sharon Edgar, whom I last saw when I was twelve. Thank you to Publisher David Stevens of the Clovis *Eastern New Mexico News,* who wrote a column about my research after my visit to Farwell and gave me encouragement in finding a publisher. He even printed an account of my research, which seemed to generate some interest among his readers and encouraged me to continue polishing this manuscript.

Thank you, people of Farwell. You helped me form a mental picture of your town in 1926. I am deeply grateful to journalists who covered this story about George Hassell when it happened so many years ago. I suspect you had far more in your notebooks than the few paragraphs of copy that ended up being published in your newspapers. I have so many unanswered questions about the trial and the case, and even though I hate being scooped on such a big story, I wish you had written more on George Hassell's two family murders. I salute all the police officers of Llano Estacado country for keeping George Hassell from being lynched while continuing to investigate this murder case. I am saddened your police reports were lost or destroyed years ago.

TIMELINE OF MURDER CASE OF GEORGE J. HASSELL

1883: Thomas Hassell born in Texas.

1885: Susan Ferguson born in Oklahoma.

1888: George J. Hassell born in Texas.

1896: Ethel Ferguson, author's grandmother, born in Texas.

1901: George Hassell's mother dies.

1902: Susan and Thomas marry in Burnett, Texas.

1905: George Hassell's father dies.

1905: George Hassell sentenced to two years in state prison in Texas for embezzling funds.

1907: George Hassell enlists in Army under alias George Stovall; deserts nine months later.

1907: George Hassell marries briefly Minnie Lofley, first of reported six wives. Marriage does not last long; she later gives birth to George's son, whom he only sees once from a distance.

1907: George Hassell enlists in Navy, probably another alias, and quickly deserts in San Francisco.

1907-10: Hassell serves three years in federal prison, probably for desertion.

1910: Hassell enlists in Army but deserts again. Hassell meets Marie Vogel in San Angelo, Texas, and travels with her to California with her young son.

1915: Hassell is suspected in the murder of a man in Chicago, and Vogel is seen with him. They return to California, and adopt two children.

1916: Author's mother, Bonnie Belle Beagle, is born in Texas.

1917: Exact date unknown, but Hassell later admits to murdering Marie Vogel and three children, and burying them at a home they rented in Whittier, Calif. Neighbors believe Hassell left for San Francisco.

1920: Neighbors tell police Hassell returned to Whittier. Pay receipts later show he worked also in Fresno, Calif.., during that time frame.

1917-24: Hassell joined and served in Merchant Marine.

1924: Thomas Hassell dies of injuries suffered in farming accident on July 3rd in Blair, Okla. Susan finds and contacts George Hassell in New Orleans just before he ships out in Merchant Marine to help her with farm and children. He spends time farming and then heads to Kansas. Susan calls again for his help. Four months after her husband is killed, Susan marries George, probably sometime in November.

1924-25: Ferguson clan meets George Hassell at annual family reunions and don't like his drinking and loutish behavior.

1925: Unknown date, but Susan and George move to Farwell, Texas to farm on leased land.

1925-26: Susan's eldest child, Nora and husband, visit from California, causing a family problem with Susan's precocious daughter Maudie.

1926: In August, Susan takes Maudie to doctor in Farwell three times and discovers she is pregnant. During following months, Maudie's pregnancy causes family turmoil with George threatening to leave.

1926: Between Dec. 2 to 6, witnesses unsure when, George kills Susan and seven children. A Sunday, probably Dec. 11, Aldon returns from job in Clovis, N.M. and finds his mom and siblings gone. Hassell cooks dinner, and they go to bed. At 4

A.M. next morning, Hasssell admits to using his shotgun to kill Aldon as he sleeps.

1926, Dec. 14: witness states he sees Hassell burning things in huge bonfire at his home.

Dec. 20: witness states he bought Hassell's crops and took over lease of his home and moved in, letting Hassell sleep in a room until he can move.

Dec. 22: Hassell conducts auction with many attending and sells all his possessions. People unwittingly walk over the buried remains of the Hassell family in covered pit.

Dec. 23: Authorities summon and question Hassell about his missing family that has aroused suspicion among neighbors. He claims his family is out of town but offers conflicting and suspicious statements.

Dec. 24: Hassell attempts suicide and is taken to Clovis, hospital. He admits murder and later provides a sworn confession.

Dec. 29: Judge orders grand jury to hear evidence against Hassell, as thousands crowd town and threaten to lynch Hassell. He is moved from jail to jail as trial nears.

1927: On Jan. 4 Jury returns indictment of nine counts of murder. On Jan. 7, Hassell enters plea and his attorney is appointed. On Jan. 10, trial convenes and concludes Jan. 11. Early Jan. 12, after two hours of deliberations, jury convicts Hassell.

On Feb. 25, Hassell is sentenced to the electric chair.

1928, After appeals are denied, Hassell is executed on Feb. 10.

1973: Last of Susan's family, daughter Nora, dies in Hemet, Calif.

2012: Author's mother dies.

NOTES

7 Testimony of N.A. Lindop, State of Texas v. George J. Hassell

10 *History of Parmer County, Texas*, Parmer County Historical Society, 1974, Pg. 67

15 Today in History. www.thepeoplehistory.com

17 Testimony of Parmer County Sheriff James Martin, State of Texas v. George J. Hassell

18 Associated Press, *Whittier Press*, Dec. 31, 1926, *Lonely Graves: A Texas Murder Trilogy*, Lana Payne Barnett, 2013, George J. Hassell confession, State of Texas v. George J. Hassell.

24 Testimony of Nora Gigler, State of Texas v. George J. Hassell

25 Obituary, Nora Parker, *Hemet News*, 1973.

27 Testimony of Sheriff James Martin, State of Texas v. George J. Hassell

28 "Understanding the Insanity Defense," Texas District & County Attorneys Association, *The Texas Prosecutor*, May-June 2021.

30 George J. Hassell confession, State of Texas v. George J. Hassell

31 Interview by Warden, *El Paso Times*, Feb. 4, 1928

34 Diaries of Ethel Beagle and Bonnie Churchill; family history and genealogy records of Ferguson clan, commissioned in 1970s.

35 Multiple witnesses testimony in State of Texas v. George J. Hassell

38 Four-part anniversary series *Abilene Globe News,* December 1976

43 Brief for State, George J. Hassell Appellant v. State of Texas, 1928

54 Transcript of State of Texas v. George J. Hassell, Texas Archives

192 *Sedalia Democrat*, Sedalia, Missouri, Jan. 14, 1927

196 Interviews Robert DeLong, 2018, and Dr. Tammy McCoy-Arballo, 2021

198 "What Drives a Man to Kill His Own Family? Inside the Psychology of Family Annihilators," *Rolling Stone,* March 8, 2019. Interview with Dr. Melanie Malterer, 2021.

199 Brief to the State of Texas, Appellant George J. Hassell, Texas Archives

215 *History of Parmer County, Texas*, Parmer County Historical Society

218 *The Flamboyant Judge, James D. Hamlin*, as told to J. Everts Haley and Wm. Curry Holden, 1972

224 *The Rope, the Chair & the Needle, Capital Punishment in Texas, 1923-1990,* James W. Marquart, Sheldon Ekland-Olson and Jonathan R. Sorenson

www.ingramcontent.com/pod-product-compliance
Lightning Source LLC
LaVergne TN
LVHW052307200926
848481LV00002B/490
9798888122396